YOU READ?

"You shall not add to the word that I speak to you, neither shall you take away from it: keep the commandments of the Lord your God which I command you."

—Deuteronomy 4:2

WHICH BIBLE SHOULD YOU READ?

By

Thomas A. Nelson

"Every word of God is fire tried: he is a buckler to them that hope in him. Add not any thing to his words, lest thou be reproved, and found a liar."

—Proverbs 30:5-6

TAN BOOKS AND PUBLISHERS, INC.
Rockford, Illinois 61105

ISBN 0-89555-689-8

Library of Congress Control No.: 00-134741

Printed and bound in the United States of America.

TAN BOOKS AND PUBLISHERS, INC.
P.O. Box 424
Rockford, Illinois 61105
2001

Dedicated to
The Blessed Virgin Mary,
"full of grace,"

"Mother of fair love, and of fear, and of knowledge, and of holy hope,"

Who shall crush the head of Satan.

Contents

PREFACE

Which Bible should you read? That is an important question everyone should ask himself. For version differs from version of Sacred Scripture by so much that one has to recognize that they cannot all be accurate—if indeed, logically speaking, any one of them is. Therefore, which one should a person choose to use for his own personal study of God's Holy Word?

In order to shed some light on this question the reader is asked initially to consider a most unusual letter that was mailed to this publisher in 1985, a letter which describes one person's singular, prayerful quest to discover that one Bible translation which is the best version to read in English. It was written by a nun who gave us permission to reprint it, and it is given here *in toto*, just as it came to us. It is addressed to the Publisher as a result of her reading a promotional sales letter the company mailed out in 1985, which outlined briefly the chief reasons for employing the traditional English Catholic Bible, called the *Douay-Rheims*. Here is her unusual story.

A Testimony

October 20, 1985

Dear Mr. Nelson:

Your Letter in regard to the Douay-Rheims Version of the Bible was absolutely fascinating. And after I finished, I wished that I could read more. Have you thought of doing a full length work on the subject? You write so beautifully.

But on the mystical side, I thought I might share my own story with you:

I grew up in the Methodist Church, but was hungry for a deeper spirituality, particularly contemplative. In 1962 I studied with a Hindu guru and later also studied other areas of Eastern contemplation. I was fascinated with Eastern mysticism and contemplation and never would have thought of leaving it. But Jesus just scooped me up like a little lamb about his shoulders, and I converted to Catholicism in 1972. So that was ten years in which I was immersed in "New Age" circles and Eastern mysticism. (In fact, my guru gave me the name of Shiva Kumari, and I'd had it changed legally, which is why Cardinal O'Connor left it as it was when he pronounced my vows as a hermit nun.)

When I first converted to Catholicism 14 years ago, I was so *lost!* I had no idea there was such a thing as "left wing" and "right wing" [in the Catholic Church]. I just wanted to learn the teachings of the Faith. But one priest said one thing; someone else said the opposite; and I became terribly confused. So I turned back to prayer.

Then I went to bookstores, but since I had no concept of that which was orthodox and that which was not, I bought books indiscriminately and became even more confused! So I turned back to prayer.

Through prayer and continually throwing myself upon the Lord, depending wholly upon Him, looking to Him in all my need and confusion, He has led me out of the darkness into the Light. I look back now over those many years and am absolutely amazed at how He has led me! But I think the *Douay-Rheims* story is most awesome:

When I first converted and was going from one Catholic bookstore to another, I picked up different versions of the Bible, not having the foggiest notion as to which would be the best. I finally concluded that they must all be good, so I got copies of each. And I already had the *King James Version* from my Protestant days.

(I'm sitting here trying to think how I can capsulize 20 years of spiritual growth and transformation which enabled me to be able to listen to the Lord on that mystical level and allow Him to guide me—most of it is grace though—all glory and honor to Him!)

What happened was odd indeed—when I picked up the *New American Version*, it was dry like sawdust. There was no life in it; I mean mystical life. (I'm having such a difficult time verbalizing this, since it was all interior guidance on a mystical level.) So I stopped trying to read the *New American*. Then I tried another version, and the words literally swam on the page. I thought I might be suffering from some sort of eye strain, so I stopped reading that version.

Finally, someone suggested the *Douay-Rheims*. I'd never even heard of such a thing, but wrote down the words and went immediately to a bookstore that carried it. (I guess this was about 10 years ago.) The minute I touched the *Douay-Rheims*, I knew this was it! I stood there in the book-store, turning it about in my hand (without ever opening it) just feeling that wonderful sensation of life which seemed to be coursing through it. (I've never told this story to anyone! They would think I was completely "off-the-wall"!)

I got my *Douay-Rheims* home, and oh, what a happy day! I've loved that book as though it were not a book at all, because that sensation of life has never left it. Whenever I touch it, and certainly when I read it, everything comes alive with God's light, love and guidance.

A couple of years ago, a man said I ought to read the St. Joseph's version, and I said I intended to stick to my *Douay-Rheims*—with a tone that sounded as though I were defending my best friend—and I couldn't give any rational explanation as to why I felt that way. I never doubted that it was the hand of the Lord; it's just that I hadn't really given it any thought until I read your letter. Then all these incidents flooded back into my memory, and I was struck with wonder!

God bless you,

Sister Shiva Kumari

Abbreviations of the Bible Versions Used in this Tract

Catholic

DRB	Douay-Rheims Bible
NAB	New American Bible
CRSV	Catholic Revised Standard Version
JB	Jerusalem Bible

Protestant

KJV	King James Version
NKJV	New King James Version
NIV	New International Version
NRSV	New Revised Standard Version
NASV	New American Standard Version
NEB	New English Bible

INTRODUCTION

The present little book is an unabashed apologia* for the traditional Catholic Bible in English, called the *Douay-Rheims*. The first edition of this present little work was actually a sales letter promoting the *Douay-Rheims Bible* by explaining to readers why the *Douay-Rheims* is the most accurate and most reliable version of the Bible in English.

This version of Sacred Scripture was first published in the New Testament at Rheims in Northern France in 1582 and at Douay in Flanders (Northwestern France) in 1609-1610 in its entirety. (These were the times of the penal laws in England under Elizabeth I, when it was a capital crime to practice the Catholic faith. Thus, the work of rendering into English a proper Bible translation had to be carried out on the Continent.) It was later revised (1749-1751) by Bishop Richard Challoner (1691-1781), Coadjutor Roman Catholic Bishop of London from 1741 and Vicar Apostolic from 1758. A slight revision was made in 1859

---

*"*Apologia*" is used here in the sense of "a defense."

by Mgr. F. P. Kenrick, Archbishop of Baltimore, which is commonly used in the United States, though other *Douay-Rheims* versions have been in use. The current edition in print by TAN was issued in 1899 by the John Murphy Co. of Baltimore, Maryland, under the official approbation of His Eminence, James Cardinal Gibbons, dated September 1, 1899, wherein he stated: "We hereby approve of the publication by Messrs. John Murphy Co. of the Catholic Bible, which is an accurate reprint of the Rheims and Douay edition with Dr. Challoner's notes."

From the first edition of the *Douay-Rheims Bible* in 1609-1610 until 1941, there was no other English Catholic Bible in use, and even until approximately 1960 the readings from the pulpit in most Catholic churches in the U.S. continued to be from the *Douay-Rheims* because there existed a popular, large-print lectionary of the Epistles and Gospels for each Sunday of the year that was in common use in most Catholic parishes in this country; it used the *Douay-Rheims* translation. Therefore, one might say that the universal use of the *Douay-Rheims Bible* lasted from Bishop Challoner's revisions in 1749-51 until approximately 1960, roughly some 210 years. But, if one were to begin from the original issue date of the first edition of the *Douay-Rheims* in 1610 until 1960, the time span of the effective, universal life of this version is 350 years.

Thus, the *only* Catholic version of the Bible in use in the English-speaking world for 330 years (c. 1610-1940) was the *Douay-Rheims*, which continued to be used for pulpit readings for about 20 years more. There was a hiatus of its availability for about 10 years, until 1971, when the *Douay-Rheims* was first issued by TAN. Even during *this* period (1960-1971), however, there were other English editions of the *Douay-Rheims* available here and there from older inventories.

The important point to consider from this brief historical sketch is that for 330 years (1610-1940), English-speaking Catholics had *no other* English Catholic Bible than the *Douay-Rheims*, and therefore, if this version is not accurate, then all the many millions of Catholics who used it since 1610—as of this writing a time span now of 390 years—have been deceived in their study of Scripture. They have not, in effect, had an accurate version of God's Holy Word. The Holy Ghost, in other words, had let them down, had failed them in their Scripture study; they have been, to a fairly large degree, deluded by a "bad" bible.

The above is also a correct line of reasoning if we compare the *Douay-Rheims* version with the three modern Catholic Bibles currently in use, namely, *The New American Bible* (1970, which was partially revised and reissued in 1986), *The Catholic Revised Standard Version* (1966, originally a Protestant Version dating from 1946 and 1952) and the *Jerusalem Bible* (1966). If any one of these three translations of Scripture is correct (and they all differ among themselves), then the *Douay-Rheims* is simply inaccurate. *But,* if the *Douay-Rheims* is accurate, then these new Catholic versions contain many inaccurate passages and should not be used. A number of comparisons between the *Douay-Rheims* and these newer Catholic versions shall be made further along in this work. These comparisons shall also include several popular Protestant versions.

In this little tract we shall study in depth 11 famous passages from the New Testament and mention two from the Old Testament. The rationale for this approach in using mainly New Testament passages is to eliminate any objections based on the original Hebrew texts of the Old Testament, the reasoning being this: If the translators of these new Bibles cannot translate correctly even the extant "original" Greek text of the New Testament—for the New Testament was written in that language*—then how are we to trust them to translate accurately the ancient Hebrew texts, which by reason of age and antiquity are far more arcane and often are far more poetic and filled with double and triple entendre?

Here a word needs to be said about the use of Hebrew in the Old Testament of the Bible. The ancient Hebrew in which most of the Old Testament was written is an ancient Semitic language that has come down to us from time immemorial. Some think Hebrew was the language spoken by man at the time of the multiplication of languages, caused by God as a curse on mankind because of man's trying to build the Tower of Babel. (*Genesis* 11:1-9).

In the course of the centuries, Hebrew

*It has been commonly held that St. Matthew's Gospel was written in Aramaic. However, no copy of the Aramaic has survived. Current thinking holds that it is not certain that he did not in fact write his Gospel in Greek.

was discontinued as a spoken language—about the time of the Babylonian Captivity in the 6th century B.C. (599-536)—when it was superseded by Aramaic. Thereafter, Hebrew was only written. Nonetheless, the Hebrew of the Old Testament texts displays a great fixity over a number of centuries that is admirable and quite unparalleled in most other languages—which tend to mutate more. This relative stability of Hebrew was inspired, no doubt, by Almighty God to preserve the integrity of the Old Testament's original language.

As a result of Alexander the Great's 4th-century conquest (334-323 B.C.) of the land of Israel, Egypt and Mesopotamia, among other areas, the spread of Greek influence and language by the 3rd century B.C. caused Ptolemy II Philadelphus, King of Egypt (284-247 B.C.), to bring to Alexandria, Egypt, 72 Hebrew scholars to translate "the Law"—presumably the Pentateuch, or first five books of the Bible—into Greek (284 B.C.). This version became known as the "Septuagint" (from the *seventy*-two scholars) and is one of the basic versions of Scripture; the entire Greek text of Old Testament Scripture is presumed not to have been the work of the original 72 men, but to have been completed during many following years. Nonetheless, the Greek of the Septuagint—called *koine* (pronounced *koinay*)—is the Greek spoken at that time by the Jews of Alexandria, Egypt, and the Greek Septuagint text of the Old Testament is one of the most venerable and accurate texts of the Old Testament we have.

Most of the Old Testament's 45 books were originally written in Hebrew, and it is generally thought all of the New Testament's 27 books were written in Greek, save for St. Matthew's Gospel, which was thought for many years to have been originally written in Aramaic, though the Aramaic text has been lost to history, even if this is so.

Approximately 150 A.D., a version of the entire Bible in Latin was assembled, called the *Old Itala (Vetus Itala)*. It was in general use until St. Jerome translated the Bible into Latin (390-405), this latter being called the *Latin Vulgate*, which was written in the "vulgar" or common Latin tongue. This version soon superseded the *Old Itala* version and is now considered an august, sacred translation in its own right, having received the approbation, not only of nearly 16 centuries of continuous use, but also formally by the Council of Trent (1545-1563), which means, as Pope Pius XII has stated, that it is free from doctrinal error. (See page 4.) The Vulgate has served the Western Catholic Church ever since and was used exclusively until modern vernacular translations began to appear in the 15th and 16th centuries.

WHICH BIBLE SHOULD YOU READ?

The Importance of the *Latin Vulgate Bible*

To begin, the *Douay-Rheims Bible* is an absolutely faithful translation into English of the *Latin Vulgate Bible*, which St. Jerome (342-420) translated into Latin *from the original languages.* The Vulgate quickly became the *only* Bible universally used in the Western Church, or the Latin Rite (by far the largest rite of the Catholic Church, spread virtually worldwide). St. Jerome, who was one of the four Great Western Fathers of the Catholic Church, was a man raised up by God to translate the Holy Bible into the common Latin of his day.

He was Greek-speaking from birth, and being an educated man, he also knew Latin perfectly, speaking it as we do English; he also knew Hebrew and Aramaic nearly as well (he studied Hebrew, e.g., from approximately age 26 as a penance). He even learned Chaldaic just so he could check the translation of the *Book of Daniel* (the only biblical book written in that language), which he had commissioned someone else to translate for him. He lived at Bethlehem and was near enough to the Rabbinical school at Caesarea-Philipi that he could consult with one of the learned Rabbis, who agreed to help him with his Hebrew—though rendering such help was actually forbidden in Jewish custom. He became so good at translating Hebrew that at the age of 70 or so he translated the book of *Tobias* in one night. Besides being a towering linguistic genius, he was also a great Saint, **and he had access to ancient Hebrew and Greek manuscripts of the 2nd and 3rd centuries which have since perished and are no longer available to scholars today.**

St. Jerome's translation, moreover, was (wherever possible) a careful, word-for-word rendering of the original texts into Latin. To quote one writer, "His sources being both numerous and ancient, his knowledge of the languages a living knowledge, his scholarship consummate, he was a far better judge of the true shade of meaning of a particular word than any modern scholar . . ." (Ronald D. Lambert, *Experiment in Heresy, Triumph Mag.*, March, 1968). Or, one might add, than any modern scholar *could ever hope to be!*

Truly, God raised up for the Church this great, great man, that He might, through him, give us a faithful rendering of His Divine Word into Latin—which was, until only 200 years ago, the universal language of all Western Christendom and which is still today the official language of the Catholic Church. Latin, moreover, as with Greek, is still taught in most major colleges and universities in the Western World, which makes the *Vulgate* easily accessible to scholars throughout the world yet today.

St. Jerome's *Latin Vulgate Bible* has been read and honored by the Western Church *for almost 1600 years*! It was declared by the Council of Trent (1545-1564) to be the official (literally "authentic") version of the canonical Scriptures, that is, **the Bible** of the Catholic Church. Hear what that Sacred Council decreed:

"Moreover, the same Holy Council . . . ordains and declares that the old Latin Vulgate Edition, which, in use for so many hundred years, has been approved by the

Church, be in public lectures, disputations, sermons and expositions held as authentic, and that no one [may] dare or presume under any pretext whatsoever to reject it." (Fourth Session, April 8, 1546).

As Pope Pius XII has stated in his 1943 encyclical letter *On The Promotion of Biblical Studies,* this means that the Vulgate, "interpreted in the sense in which the Church has always understood it," is "**free from any error whatsoever in matters of faith and morals;** so that, as the Church herself testifies and affirms, it may be quoted safely and without fear of error in disputations, in lectures and in preaching . . ." (Par. 21). No other Bible—not even the *New Vulgate*, promulgated in 1979, and not yet available in English—has been endorsed by the Church in this manner!

The Stature of the *Vulgate* and *Douay-Rheims* Bibles

The reason that the *Douay-Rheims Bible* is so important is that it is the only English Bible that is a faithful, word-for-word translation of the Latin Vulgate of St. Jerome. This absolute fidelity to the Vulgate has always been

its claim, and no one denies that it is so! The obvious conclusion to be drawn from these basic facts is that **the *Douay-Rheims Bible* is therefore the best and safest translation of the Holy Bible into English!**

Personally speaking, this writer has been reading the *Douay-Rheims Bible* for over 30 years and can attest that it literally bristles with meaning, that it is replete, verse after verse, with wonderful shades and nuances of meaning, such that no human being could possibly have written without being aided by Almighty God—and which subtleties the modern translators have often translated out of their versions. A single phrase—sometimes only a word—can deliver a key insight to the person reading the *Douay-Rheims*. This writer has never experienced anything similar while reading any other version. In comparison, all other versions seem prosaic and flat.

This characteristic makes an extremely strong argument by itself that the *Douay-Rheims* is an accurate translation of the Bible as it existed in its original languages—even though the *Douay-Rheims* is in large part a translation of a translation (i.e., English from Latin). But the wonderful subtleties of the *Douay-Rheims* are almost all lost in the other versions.

"Which Bible should you read?" It really devolves to this: If God does not guide the translation of the Bible, much of its meaning can easily be lost in translation—**which this writer believes has in fact happened to the English versions other than the *Douay-Rheims*.** It is the firm opinion of this writer that God has safely guided St. Jerome and the translators of the *Douay-Rheims Bible*, for which reason the latter is such a pithy translation, and so pregnant and charged with meaning at every turn. Comparable to the exclamations directed at the chief priests and Pharisees by the ministers sent to apprehend Jesus, who had heard Our Lord Himself: "Never did man speak like this man" (*John* 7:46); this writer is convinced, from repeated, careful, studied reading of the *Douay-Rheims Bible*, that *we* can say, "no human being, unaided by divine inspiration, could have written such a book as the *Douay-Rheims Bible*," something he could never say of any other version he has read. The *Douay-Rheims Bible* spontaneously elicits from the human heart the exclamation: **"*This* is Sacred Scripture!"**

St. Jerome and the other ancient translators rendered their translations of Scripture as much as possible in a word-for-word or expression-for-expression manner from the original manuscripts. They did not try to interpret their own understanding *into* the Bible and thereby translate for us *what they understood the meaning to be,* as the modern biblical translators often seem to have done. (This practice is fatal to an accurate translation of the Bible and in this writer's opinion is the primary reason why there are so many versions of the Bible.) Rather, the ancient translators translated the texts exactly as they found them and "let the chips fall as they may."

The *Douay-Rheims Bible,* in its own right, is *just such a translation* into English—a word-for-word, you might say *slavishly* faithful translation of the *Vulgate*, the "authentic" Bible of the Catholic Church (It is the Council of Trent that used the word "authentic.") But its translation was made by comparing it also to the transcripts of the original languages (wherever this was possible) and to the Greek Septuagint of the Old Testament.

Moreover, thousands of Catholic Saints were raised on the *Latin Vulgate* and the

Douay-Rheims Bible. Our Catholic literary heritage overflows with quotations from the *Vulgate* and the *Douay-Rheims* translation. But in the new bibles, the familiar wording of the *Douay-Rheims* is often gone, in some verses totally—and many times also the meaning!

Furthermore, the notes in the *Douay-Rheims Bible* are in total accord with the pronouncements of the Church on the true meaning of the Scriptures. *This cannot be said of all the modern bibles.* (The Preface to the *New American Bible* (NAB, '70), e.g., states that some of its collaborators were not even Catholics!)

Without the *Douay-Rheims Bible*'s being universally available and used, our Catholic Scriptural traditions in English will be lost to our children and grandchildren, as well as to future generations in the Church!

Therefore, it is the considered opinion of this writer that, if one wants the true Word of God in the English language—officially guaranteed by the Catholic Church—he or she must go to the *Douay-Rheims Bible*.

The Method of Translating Employed in the New Bibles

At this point, it is of paramount importance to explain the method of translating the Sacred Scriptures which the modern Catholic translators—from the evidence of their translations—would seem to have employed, a method which has resulted in renderings of Scripture into such *unfamiliar* language as to make a person sometimes wonder whether or not he is actually reading the Bible.

For the purposes of this booklet, discussion of the modern Catholic versions of the Bible will be confined to and refer specifically to the three most widely used translations, viz., the *New American Bible* of 1970 (which is used in the Catholic liturgy in America), and also occasionally of 1986 (here referenced as NAB, '70 or NAB, '86) ; the Catholic Edition of the *Revised Standard Version* (CRSV, '66), and the *Jerusalem Bible* of 1966 (JB, '66). **But,** because many Catholics are now using the *New King James Version* (NKJV, '85), the *New International Version* (NIV, '78), the *New Revised Standard Version* (NRSV, '89), the *New American Standard Version*

(NASV, '77) or the *New English Bible* (NEB, '76), these five will also be considered.

Three Fundamental Mistakes

In researching this subject, the present writer soon concluded that the translators of the three modern Catholic bibles currently most in use—and indeed of all the modern translations reviewed—have made three fundamental mistakes:

***First,* they have bypassed St. Jerome's Latin Vulgate version of Scripture in favor of translating transcriptions of texts in the original languages** which are not considered as trustworthy by the translators of the original *Douay-Rheims Bible* as is the *Vulgate*.

***Second,* they have often employed word meanings for their translations which, though correct in some sense of the words, are often incorrect for the particular use in which they occur in the Bible.**

***Third,* and probably worst of all, the modern translators seem to have read the original language versions of the Bible, decided in their own minds what the meaning is, and translated**

***that* meaning into English, rather than what the Bible actually says.**

Let us explain the ramifications of these three fundamental mistakes:

1. Which Authoritative "Original" To Use?

First, we do not possess *any* original manuscripts of *any* of the books of the Holy Bible. The passage of time and the deterioration of materials have caused these to be lost to us. Moreover, the texts we do have of the Hebrew and the Greek original languages do not completely agree among themselves as well as do the texts we have of the Latin Vulgate of St. Jerome.

Sometimes the question is raised: Why translate from a translation (i.e., from the Latin Vulgate), rather than from the original Greek and Hebrew? This question was also raised in the 16th century when the Douay-Rheims translators (Fr. Gregory Martin and his assistants) first published the Rheims New Testament. They gave ten reasons, ending up by stating that the Latin Vulgate "is not onely better then al other Latin translations, but then the Greeke text itselfe, in those places where they disagree." (Preface to the *Rheims New Testament*, 1582). They state that "both the Hebrew and Greeke Editions are fouly corrupted . . . since the Latin was truly translated out of them, whiles they were more pure; and that the same Latin hath been farre better conserved from corruptions." (Preface to the *Douay Old Testament*, 1609 facsimile edition published by Gordon Winrod, Our Savior's Church and Latin School, Gainesville, Mo., 1987).

What is the reason? There were always far more copies of the Vulgate made, and it has therefore been much easier to detect copyists' errors. It must be remembered here that printing from moveable type was not invented until approximately the 1430's and not really employed very much until the 1440's, when Johann Gutenberg printed a calendar in 1448 and the first Bible at Mainz, Germany in the 1450's. Prior to that, the Bible, as with all books, had to be reproduced by handwriting.

Also, it was commonly believed by the Fathers of the Church "that the Jews did corrupt the text of the Bible in order to destroy the arguments of the Christians," (cf. Hugh Pope, O.P., *Eng. Versions of the Bible*, 1952, p. 655, n. 15). They would have done this in order to disclaim Our Lord as the Messias. For example, in the Old Testament prophet *Aggeus*, 2:8 (*Haggai* 2:7 in the new bibles), we find a prophecy about Our Lord as the Messias which reads, **"And I will move all nations: AND THE DESIRED OF ALL NATIONS SHALL COME: and I will fill this house with glory: saith the Lord of hosts."** (DRB, emphasis in original).

Let us now hear what the *New American Bible* has: "I will shake all the nations, and the treasures of all the nations will come in, And I will fill this house with glory, says the LORD of hosts." (NAB, '70 & '86). The two other Catholic versions have basically the same translation, as also do the NEB, the NASV and the NRSV; only the NIV agrees with the *Douay-Rheims*; the NKJV almost does.

"The Desired of all nations" refers to Christ. "I will move all the nations" (DRB) would seem to refer to God's grace moving them to be disposed to accept Christ when He comes to them through the Catholic Church. On the other hand, "and the treasures of all the nations shall come in" (NAB, '70 & '86) appears to indicate there will be a worldwide empire that "shakes down" the nations to extort from them their wealth. Thus, a far different meaning is rendered from what the *Douay-Rheims Bible* has.

In any case, for modern scholars to go back to the transcriptions of the Hebrew and Greek, in which various books of the Bible were originally written, and make translations from these (not always reliable) transcriptions that are fundamentally different in *hundreds of different* cases from the translation rendered by St. Jerome nearly 1600 years ago (and faithfully translated by the *Douay-Rheims*) is to demand of any sensible Catholic today to reject their work completely and out of hand—and for this reason only. **For if a Catholic does not reject these new translations of the Bible, then he really has rejected the nearly 1600 years of Catholic biblical interpretation, based on the *Latin Vulgate Bible*,** and has accepted in their stead one or all of the many truncated, ersatz biblical renderings of the modern Bible translators.

Rather, and far more sensibly, Catholics should reject these questionable new "bibles" (bibles that are seemingly always being updated and corrected in ever newer editions) and return to the traditional translation of Scripture based on St. Jerome, which in English is the *Douay-Rheims Bible.*

One should remember the status of St. Jerome's translation of the Bible for the Catholic Church: **His translation is, for working purposes, in effect, THE BIBLE as far as the Church is concerned**, for it was the only Bible in universal use by the Latin Rite of the Catholic Church for some 1600 years. *And it is* ***still*** *the only "authentic" Bible of the Catholic Church* for use in sermons, lectures and theological discussions, as declared by the Council of Trent! (The Church has not clarified yet what is the status of *New Vulgate*, completed in 1979, which has not yet been translated into English.)

If the new bibles are correct in the countless ways they differ from St. Jerome's translation, then his translation is terribly flawed; therefore, the Latin Rite of the Roman Catholic Church simply has not had the Bible properly translated for more than 1600 years! **But such a situation is simply preposterous in the True Church of God, which is guided by the Holy Ghost.** For Scripture, with Tradition, forms one of the two sources of the Catholic Faith. Therefore, on the basis of concluding that the Catholic Church **must have always had** the correct translation of Scripture—its being God's Church, and Sacred Scripture being, with Tradition, one of the two sources of the supernatural True Faith—**then we are forced to concede that St. Jerome's translation is accurate** (especially as far as doctrine goes—cf. the quote from Pius XII on page 4), and that the new translations that differ from it so profoundly are not—at least to the extent that they *do* differ from it! **One simply cannot escape this conclusion.**

What is of paramount importance concerning the translation of the original Hebrew and Greek is that St. Jerome had far more texts of the original language versions to work with than scholars have today. It is commonly acknowledged that he had many texts that simply no longer exist.

Of particular importance was the *Hexapla*, assembled by Origen (c.185–c.254), a six-column Bible dating from about 240 A.D., giving the existing two Hebrew and four Greek versions of Scripture; it was a work kept at Caesarea in Palestine, near where St. Jerome worked on the Bible.

Moreover, St. Jerome was a fairly wealthy man, and he collected texts and paid copyists to copy them for him as often as he came across anything worthwhile. He simply had far more to work with than scholars have today, as far as texts go. Further, he was 1600 years closer to the original languages than modern scholars. *And* he was bilingual, speaking Greek from birth and Latin from his youth.

2. Incorrect Choice of Words

Second, regarding the meanings of the words used by the original biblical writers, who is going to be a better judge of the exact meanings of the various Hebrew and Greek words employed in Scripture: St. Jerome, who was Greek-speaking from birth, who knew Latin as well as most of us know English, and who knew Hebrew almost as well, who was also a towering linguistic genius, a great Saint, a holy Doctor of the Church, and one of the four Great Western Fathers of the Church; or, is it going to be the modern scholars, who have to learn their ancient Latin, Greek and Hebrew from grammars and lexicons, from dictionaries and from professors who (presumably) do not speak the language natively either and who themselves have thus had to learn it—and so forth, back through time, during the course of some 1600 years? **The far safer bet is St. Jerome!**

On this second point, concerning which meaning of the original words of Scripture to use in making translations, one should consider momentarily the English word "grace" and its various meanings. It can mean "supernatural life," "unmerited divine assistance," "a prayer said before meals," "an instance of human kindness," "pardon," "a reprieve," "to be in one's favor," "ease and suppleness of movement," "a charming trait," "a title of address" (e.g., "Your Grace"), etc. The same problem exists in the ancient languages, Greek and Hebrew, in which the Bible was originally written.

The translators of the modern Catholic bibles in question would seem to be choosing the wrong meaning to words in many, many instances. *Granted,* they generally do have *one* of the correct meanings of a given word in question, but have they chosen the **correct** meaning of the word in *every* instance? From the results of their translations, it would seem not—and this can be seen merely by the crazy way the passages often read when they get done.

Again, consider the word "grace"—in Greek, *charis.* As one conservative Catholic professor of Hebrew, Greek and Latin told this author, by the time St. Paul wrote, the Greek word *charis* already had its specifically Christian theological meaning of "grace." And St. Jerome corresponded to St. Paul's meaning by translating *charis* into Latin as *gratia,* which in English becomes "grace."

(Let us remember that the Septuagint—the Old Testament Bible in Greek, dating from *circa* 284 B.C.—had been rendered into that language some 300 years before St. Paul wrote, and therefore the meanings of the words St. Paul and the other New Testament writers used in the original Greek of the New Testament were already well established in most cases.)

But the translators of the *New American Bible*, for example, render *Luke* 1:28—which traditionally reads, **"Hail, full of grace, the Lord is with thee: blessed art thou among women" (DRB)**—as, "Rejoice, O highly favored daughter! . . ." (NAB, '70. The NAB, '86 has "Hail, favored one!").

It does not take any particular mental acumen to distinguish the difference between being "full of grace" and "highly favored." "Favor" or "favored" is *one* of the meanings for *charis,* but not the one intended by St. Luke in Scripture. A person may be highly favored with any number of talents and abilities, or with good looks or plenty of money, and so forth. But does that mean he or she is therefore "full of grace"? We understand Our Lady to be "full of grace" in the sense of being absolutely full of God's divine life (Sanctifying Grace), so that there is no sin in her soul whatsoever. What a difference in meanings!

3. Interpreting Rather than Translating

***And thirdly,* concerning the method of translating employed by the translators of the modern Catholic Bibles**, this writer believes it can be demonstrated clearly where they are mistaken; *and this point alone brings into question the value of their entire work.*

The ancient translators of the Sacred Scripture, by and large, did literal, word-for-word translations of the Bible. It was their policy to be faithful to every word—and to every shade of meaning of every word—used in the Bible. This included the 72 Hebrew scholars who translated the Old Testament into Greek at Alexandria, Egypt, about 284 B.C.; the translator(s) of the *Old Itala (Vetus Itala)* Latin Bible of about 150 A.D.; and of course, St. Jerome, who did the *Latin Vulgate Bible* and who finished his work about 405 A.D. The same is true of the original *Douay-Rheims* commission (1582-1610), of Bishop Richard Challoner (1748-1751), and of Mgr. Kenrick (1859).

However, the translators of the modern Catholic bibles—in the judgment of this writer, after reading their translations and comparing them to the *Douay-Rheims*, the *Vulgate* and the Greek of the New Testament—are proceeding according to the following method:

They read a text in the current transcriptions of the original languages, decide what THEY THINK it means, and then translate THEIR interpretation into English! The result is that the English is sometimes (not always!) easier to understand, but it is not necessarily what the Bible says; **rather, it is THEIR INTERPRETATION AND THEIR UN-**

DERSTANDING OF WHAT THE BIBLE SAYS! And often the difference from the *Vulgate* and DRB, the traditional Catholic versions, is glaring.

Sample Problem Passages

At this point let us consider some examples of the devastating results to Sacred Scripture from these three—what this writer believes to be—mistakes of the translators of the modern Catholic editions of the Bible. One should remember that these "mistakes," as maintained here, are 1) **the use of transcriptions from ancient texts that are questionable and that disagree with the *Latin Vulgate* of St. Jerome**, 2) **the wrong choice of meanings of words** in certain specific cases (though these poorly chosen meanings would be legitimate meanings when used in other contexts), and 3) **translating their INTERPRETATION of what the Bible means**, as opposed to translating what the Bible actually says.

"She Shall Crush Thy Head . . ."

In *Genesis* 3:15 (*Douay-Rheims Bible*) we read God's judgment against Lucifer for his part in Original Sin, as well as God's prophecy concerning him: **"I will put enmities between thee and the woman, and thy seed and her seed: she shall crush thy head, and thou shalt lie in wait for her heel." (DRB).**

All three modern Catholic translations are fundamentally different from the *Douay-Rheims*, but all basically agree with each other. First in order is the translation of the *New American Bible*, the one used in the Catholic liturgy today:

"I will put enmity between you and the woman, and between your offspring and hers; He will strike at your head, while you strike at his heel." (NAB, '70 and '86). This renders a very different meaning indeed from the *Douay-Rheims* version. Now read how the other versions render this passage:

"I will put enmity between you and the woman, and between your seed and her seed; he shall bruise your head, and you shall bruise his heel." (CRSV, '66).

"I will make you enemies of each other:

you and the woman, your offspring and her offspring. It will crush your head and you will strike its heel." (JB, '66).

"I will put enmity between you and the woman, between your brood and hers. They [note the plural] shall strike at your head, and you shall strike at their heel." (NEB, '76).

"And I will put enmity between you and the woman, and between your offspring and hers; he will crush your head, and you will strike his heel." (NIV, '78).

"And I will put enmity between you and the woman, and between your seed and her Seed; He shall bruise your head, and you shall bruise His heel." (NKJV, '85).

"I will put enmity between you and the woman, and between your offspring and hers; he will strike your head, and you will strike his heel." (NRSV, '89).

"And I will put enmity between you and the woman, and between your seed and her seed. He shall bruise you on the head, and you shall bruise him on the heel." (NASV, '77).

Note how the *Douay-Rheims* makes perfect sense, but the others are confusing. (The words literally "swim" on the page.) All of the English versions other than the *Douay-Rheims* translate this verse in a very similar manner: The JB takes the pronoun to be neuter, "it" (seemingly an indecisive "cop-out"), and the NEB takes it to be plural, referring to the woman's "brood." But most take the pronoun to be masculine, referring to Our Lord as the one to "bruise" or "crush" the head of the serpent, rather than "she," referring to Our Lady. Some may think this a "small" difference, but in fact, it is very great indeed. For, from this prophecy in the *Douay-Rheims* comes a longstanding Catholic tradition that toward the End of Time the Blessed Virgin Mary will crush the head of Satan, after her devotees have promoted her honor and devotion and directed countless prayers for her intercession during a long period of time. This ancient tradition, which is based on *Genesis* 3:15, is in danger of being relegated to the scrap-heap if we accept these non-traditional translations.

Consider what Bl. Pius IX (Pope, 1846-1878) wrote on this score in his bull *Ineffabilis Deus*, declaring the dogma of the Immaculate Conception of the Blessed Virgin Mary (December 8, 1854). After citing the writings of the Fathers of the Church and other learned writers, he concludes: "Hence, just as Christ, the Mediator between God and man, assumed human nature, blotted the handwriting of the decree that stood against us, and fastened it triumphantly to the cross, so the most holy Virgin, united with Him by a most intimate and indissoluble bond, was, with Him and through Him, eternally at enmity with the evil serpent, and most completely triumphed over him, and thus crushed his head with her immaculate foot."

The *Douay-Rheims*, following the *Vulgate*, is the only English Bible that translates this passage with "*she* shall crush" and "thou shalt lie in wait for *her* heel," the reference being to Blessed Virgin Mary's ultimately defeating the devil and his minions in a great spiritual battle, with the final victory being attributed to her intercession. Now this is exactly the traditional Catholic translation of this passage. Moreover, translated this way, the text makes perfect sense; translated the new way, **it is confusing!** One should stop here to read the passage again from the *Douay-Rheims* on page 23, paragraph 1, and see how nicely the meaning flows when it refers to the woman in both clauses, plus how meaningful the second clause is compared to the second clause in all the other translations.

In light of these new translations of *Genesis* 3:15, what is to become of this Catholic tradition about the role of the Blessed Virgin Mary in defeating the devil?—a tradition reinforced, it might be added, by Our Lady's apparition to St. Catherine Labouré in 1831, wherein she gave us the Miraculous Medal, whose image presents her standing on the world and crushing the head of a serpent with her foot. The truth of this apparition is reinforced by the presence of St. Catherine's beautiful, incorrupt body in the Chapel of the Daughters of Charity, at 140 rue de Bac in Paris, of which order she was a member. Hundreds of thousands of pilgrims visit this chapel every year to view her body, which is on open display and which is a phenomenal, on-going testimony to the truth of this apparition—and ultimately to the truth of the Catholic tradition that "**she**," the Blessed Mother, shall crush the serpent's head!

This prophecy of *Genesis* 3:15 is also depicted by millions of statues and pictures throughout the world which represent this prophesied event. Are we and our (at least) 1600-year-old tradition wrong in this regard, and are the modern biblical exegetes and translators right? Has the Church been misguided on this important point these many centuries? Was the Holy Ghost "asleep on the job" and let this "little translation error" slip by Him? Or, has Almighty God for His own good reasons allowed the modern translators to be led astray . . . and with them the poor souls who have to sift for Scripture's meaning through the tailings of their translations?

"I Am the Mother of Fair Love . . ."

Now, let us consider *Ecclesiasticus* 24:24-31 (*Sirach* in the new bibles), verses the Church has used for centuries in her Sacred Liturgy for the various feasts of Our Lady at Mass. The most famous part is as follows:

"I am the mother of fair love, and of fear, and of knowledge, and of holy hope. In me is all grace of the way and of the truth, in me is all hope of life and of virtue. *Come over to me, all ye that desire me, and be filled with my fruits. For my spirit is sweet above honey and my inheritance above honey and the honeycomb.* My memory is unto everlasting generations. *They that eat me, shall yet hunger: and they that drink me, shall yet thirst. He that harkeneth to me, shall not be confounded: and they that work by me, shall not sin.* They that explain me shall have life everlasting." (DRB).

Now, how do the other Catholic bibles translate this passage? Well . . . you see . . . they do not exactly! Save for the JB, they leave out four verses entirely from this passage (the non-italicized words)! The italicized part is included in the NAB ('70 and '86) and the CRSV (with different wording for each version, of course); the rest is omitted in the NAB '70 and '86 and in the CRSV. All together, Chapter 24 of *Ecclesiasticus (Sirach)* has some 16 fewer verses in the NAB ('70 and '86) and 13 fewer verses in the CRSV than the *Vulgate* and DRB! (The JB has the full 47.) According to these modern translators, apparently the Church for all these centuries was wrong for using these verses that, according to them, are not even part of authentic Scripture! One is forced to ask himself, "How much do they expect us to swallow before we say, 'Enough already!'"

One is reminded of the solemn decree of the Council of Trent issued in 1546: "If anyone does not accept as sacred and canonical the aforesaid [72] books in their entirety and with all their parts, as they have been accustomed to be read in the Catholic Church and as they are contained in the old Latin Vulgate Edition, and knowingly and deliberately rejects the aforesaid traditions, let him be anathema." (*Canons and Decrees of the Council of Trent,* Sess. IV, "Decree concerning the Canonical Scriptures," April 8, 1546).

"Wheresoever the Body Shall Be . . ."

A very unusual verse appears in *Matthew* 24:28, which occurs in the midst of Our Lord's description and prophecies about the "consummation of the world." (This verse is in the Gospel reading for the Last Sunday after Pentecost in the Traditional Latin Rite Liturgy.) Our Lord has been describing all the terrible things that are to come to pass at that time, when seemingly "out of the blue" appears this incredible verse: **"Wheresoever the body shall be, there shall the eagles also be gathered**

together." (DRB). (*Matt*. 24:28).

What does it mean? Cast in the future tense, it is a prophecy: "body" refers to: the Eucharistic Body of Christ, which at the End of Time will not be found just everywhere. For we know that Antichrist will take away the Perpetual Sacrifice (cf. *Daniel* 8:11-14), and we know that the Great Apostasy will have occurred that was mentioned by St. Paul in *2 Thessalonians* 2:3. Also, we know that Our Lord asked the Apostles, "But yet the Son of man, when he cometh, shall he find, think you, faith on earth?" (*Luke* 18:8), which would imply an answer of "No" and that therefore the Mass would be very scarce. But where the Mass *is* found, where the Eucharistic Body of Christ *is* located, "there shall the eagles," the Saints of the Catholic Church, be gathered together, for these people alone understand *spiritually*, and in the eyes of God they soar above the rest of mankind like eagles with sharp eyesight and a wide perspective of the true meaning of human existence; whereas, most people, interested only in the things of this world, grovel about on the ground, hindered by a spiritual myopia—if not indeed being totally blind to the true meaning of man's existence. (Such is also very much the gist of St. Alphonsus Liguori's traditional analysis of this verse in Chapter 21 of *Visits to the Blessed Sacrament*. St. Alphonsus—1696-1797—was a Doctor of the Church.)

The eagle, moreover, feeds on living flesh. And what did Our Lord say of His Eucharistic Body: "My flesh is meat indeed" (*John* 6:56); "I am the living bread which came down from Heaven" (*John* 6:51); etc. Plus, the eagle is a war bird and the sign of the soldier. Now the Catholic Church on earth is the Church Militant, the Church fighting—as soldiers of Christ.

All this meaning comes forth out of one short, compact verse of Scripture! And a person can see from this one short verse just how very rich, how poetic, how incredibly powerful the Bible can be, even in English . . . when properly translated!

But now, how do the new bibles translate this beautiful and consoling prophecy of Our Lord? Just consider the following:

"Where the carcass lies, there the vultures gather." (NAB, '70).

"Wherever the corpse is, there the vultures will gather." (NAB, '86).

"Wherever the body is, there the eagles will be gathered together." (CRSV, '66).

"Wherever the corpse is, there will the vultures gather." (JB, '66).

"Wherever there is a carcass, there the vultures will gather." (NIV, '78).

"Wherever the corpse is, there the vultures will gather." (NRSV, '89).

"For wherever the carcass is, there the eagles will be gathered together." (NKJV, '85).

"Wherever the corpse is, there the vultures will gather." (NASV, '77).

"Wherever the corpse is, there the vultures will gather." (NEB, '76).

Gone is the prophecy! Gone is the poetry! Gone the beautiful symbolism! Gone are the consolation and the hope! And in their place? At best a trite little truism. But when read in the context of *Matthew* 24, these new translations, save for the CRSV, have no meaning at all. Worded in the traditional way, however, the verse is rich and redolent with meaning, as seen above.

Only the Catholic Edition of the *Revised Standard Version* translates the passage correctly; whereas, all the others do not. (However, the CRSV makes errors in other passages, as we shall observe further along.)

St. Jerome's *Latin Vulgate* translates this verse: "*Ubicumque* (Wherever) *fuerit* (it will be) *corpus* (the body) *illic* (there) *congregabuntur* (shall be gathered) *et* (also) *aquilae* (eagles)." It is pretty hard to mistake *aquilae*; it simply means "eagles." The Greek original says: "*hópou èán* (Wheresoever) *ẽ* (shall be) *tò* (the) *ptõma* (body), *èkei* (there) *sunachthésontai* (shall be gathered) *hoi* (the) *àetoí* (eagles). *Aetophóros* in Greek, for example, means a "standard-bearer," literally, the "eagle-bearer," the one who carries the eagle (comparable to *Christophóros*, "Christ-bearer," from which we have the name Christopher).

Ancient armies would not have been caught dead mounting a vulture on their standards. If *àetoi* were "vultures," the Greek-speaking St. Jerome would surely have called them "vultures." If we today know what vultures are, you can be sure St. Jerome did! He was a man so eminent he was almost elected Pope when his friend, Pope St. Damasus I (366-384), died.

"Let All Your Things Be Done in Charity"

But there are other instances as well which show the glaring differences between the *Douay-Rheims Version* and the three modern Catholic versions of the Bible. Consider the following:

The *New American Bible*, the *Jerusalem Bible* and the *Catholic Revised Standard Version* (being new Catholic bibles) all substitute the word "love" for "charity," for example, in *1 Corinthians* 16:14, St. Paul says, **"Let all your things be done in charity." (DRB).** Whereas, the others say,

"Do everything with *love*." (NAB, '70).

"Your every act should be done with *love*." (NAB, '86).

"Let all that you do be done in *love*." (CRSV, '66).

"Let everything you do be done in *love*." (JB, '66).

"Let all *that* you *do* be done with *love*." (NKJV, '85).

"Do everything in *love*." (NIV, '78).

"Let all that you do be done in *love*." (NRSV, '89).

"Let all that you do be done in *love*." (NASV, '77).

"Let all you do be done in love." (NEB, '76). (Emphasis added to all quotes above.)

In Latin, it reads: "*Omnia* (all [things]) *vestra* (your) *in* (in) *charitate* (charity) *fiant* (let [them] be done)." (*Latin Vulgate*). In Greek, it reads: "*Pánta* (all things) *humōn* (your) *èn* (in) *ȁgápe* (charity) *ginéstho* (let [them] be done)." (Liddell-Scott's Lexicon of 1889 gives "love" as the translation for *ȁgápe*, but in the sense of "esp. *brotherly love, charity*; *the love of God for man and of man for God*. N.T."—Page 4). Therefore, "charity" best translates this type of "love."

The Greek word for human love is *philía*, for sexual love is *'éros*, but for divine love it is *ȁgápe*; now, St. Paul used *ȁgápe*, which St. Jerome translated as *charitas,* which in English is *charity.* The Greek *philía* becomes in Latin *amor* and in English *love*. "Charity" in the Catholic sense is "divine love"—love of God for man, love of man for God, and love of man for his fellow men, out of love for God—and "charity," moreover, has a connotation of being tempered with justice and truth; and when referring to man, it includes his being in the state of

Sanctifying Grace. The English word *"love,"* however, simply does not convey this fuller meaning.

One has to wonder how so many versions of the Bible can all agree to be wrong on the translation of this one common word in the Bible—but a word denoting the most important Christian virtue, namely *charity*.

"Amen, Amen, I Say to You . . ."

The Hebrew word *amen* has been brought over into Greek, into Latin and into English, because there is simply no equivalent to it in any other language. It has a meaning of solemnly calling the hearer to witness the truth of what is about to be said, and in the New Testament only Our Lord used it. The *Douay-Rheims Version* retains it, but the modern Catholic versions bend over backwards to *translate* it, although it is truly untranslatable and is already a bona fide English word. Witness *John* 8:58:

"Amen, amen I say to you, before Abraham was made, I am." (DRB). Now consider the three new Catholic versions and the Protestant versions:

"I solemnly declare it: before Abraham came to be, I AM." (NAB, '70).

"Truly, truly, I say to you, before Abraham was, I am." (CRSV, '66).

"I tell you most solemnly, before Abraham ever was, I Am." (JB, '66).

"Most assuredly, I say to you, before Abraham was, I AM." (NKJV, '85).

"I tell you the truth, . . . before Abraham was born, I am." (NIV, '78).

"Truly, truly, I say to you, before Abraham was born, I am!" (NASV, '77).

"Very truly, I tell you, before Abraham was, I am." (NRSV, '89).

"In very truth I tell you, before Abraham was born, I am." (NEB, '76).

"Amen, amen, I say to you" has a power the other translations do not even approach. (By the way, notice the powerful contrast in the *Douay-Rheims Bible* between "was made," regarding Abraham, and "I am," regarding God; the other translations miss this subtlety also. The Greek *genesthaí* comes from *gígnomai* and means "to come into being," according to Liddell-Scott, p. 164, and thus "to be made," which St. Jerome translates as *fieret* ("to come to be"), meaning literally, "was made." That is why the *Douay-Rheims* translates this verb as "was made."

Now consider the 1986 version of the *New American Bible*: "Amen, amen, I say to you, before Abraham came to be, I AM." (NAB, '86). This new version is almost identical to the *Douay-Rheims*, except to translate *genesthaí* as "came to be," rather than "was made." Apparently the *New American Bible* translators *have* been listening to some criticism of their work.

"Being of One Mind One Towards Another"

Now let us look at *Romans* 12:16 where St. Paul says, **"Being of one mind one towards another."** (DRB). The four new Catholic versions say,

"Have the same attitude toward all." (NAB, '70).

"Have the same regard for one another." (NAB, '86).

"Live in harmony with one another." (CRSV, '66).

"Treat everyone with equal kindness." (JB, '66).

The five Protestant versions read as follows:

"Be of the same mind toward one another." (NKJV, '85).

"Live in harmony with one another." (NIV, '78).

"Live in harmony with one another." (NRSV, '89).

"Be of the same mind toward one another." (NASV, '77).

"Care as much about each other as about yourselves." (NEB, '76)

The *New King James Version* and the *New American Standard Version* are comparable to the *Douay-Rheims* and the rest are identical to each other.

The Greek is clearer than the Latin in this verse and is easier to translate. The Latin is very compressed and takes a good knowledge of that language to see the meaning, which is much clearer in the original Greek. The Vulgate reads: "*Idipsum* (The same thing) *invicem* (mutually, reciprocally, one to another) *sentientes* (thinking, feeling)." Just three Latin words! In Greek it reads: "*Tò* (The) *aùtò* (same) *ẻis* (towards) *àllḗlous* (one another) *phronoũntes* (being of a mind, being like-minded)."

Both the Greek original and the Latin of St. Jerome use a participle ("being minded the same," "thinking the same"), rather than the imperative (or commanding) form of the verb, which is used in **all** the English translations above, except the *Douay-Rheims*, which retains the participial form of the verb ("being"). This change from the participle to the imperative form of the verb is a pure invention on the part of the modern translators. If the original uses a participle, the translation should also use it. If one will look at the Greek transliteration given above, he will see that it matches virtually perfectly with the *Douay-Rheims* translation. This is an excellent example of the extreme precision with which the *Douay-Rheims Bible* is translated—not just from the *Latin Vulgate* alone, but from the Greek "original" as well. This verse is something of a snarl to translate from the Latin, but the *Douay-Rheims* does it admirably, retaining both the meaning and the wording of the Greek "original."

The three Catholic translations are all different! Is it the same book being translated? There is a BIG difference between our "being of one mind one towards another" and the other translations. *The first is mutual,* a fact clearly indicated in the Greek "original" and in St. Jerome's *Vulgate*; it pertains to the way Christians are to behave toward each other, since we are "one body in Christ." (*Rom.* 12:5).

Christians are enjoined by St. Paul in *Ephesians* 4:3-6, "to keep the *unity* of the Spirit . . . *One* body and *one* spirit . . . in *one* hope . . . *One* Lord, *one* faith, *one* baptism. *One* God and Father of all . . ." (DRB). (Emphasis added). In other words, there is only One Body of Christ, only one True Religion of God—there *cannot* be many. Therefore, the clear meaning implied in *Romans* 12:16 is that *there is only one True Church!* And we Christians should be of "one mind, one towards another" because we are all of one belief, one philosophy and one theology, all members of the Mystical Body of Christ. The *Douay-Rheims* translation here expresses the concept perfectly because it translates the "original" Greek perfectly. From this short passage alone, one can begin to understand the ramifications of these seemingly "little" changes made in the modern English bibles.

"And the Gates of Hell Shall Not Prevail Against It."

Most people are familiar with *Matthew* 16:18-19 where Our Lord says, **"And I say to thee: That thou art Peter; and upon this rock I will build my church, and the gates of hell shall not prevail against it." (DRB).** Whereas the four new Catholic versions say,

" . . . and the jaws of death shall not prevail against it." (NAB, '70).

" . . . and the gates of the netherworld shall not prevail against it." (NAB, '86).

" . . . and the powers of death shall not prevail against it." (CRSV, '66).

" . . . And the gates of the underworld can never hold out against it." (JB, '66).

The five Protestant versions say,

" . . . and the gates of Hades shall not prevail against it." (NKJV, '85).

" . . . and the gates of Hades will not overcome it." (NIV, '78).

". . . and the gates of Hades will not prevail against it." (NRSV, '89).

" . . . and the gates of Hades shall not overpower it." (NASV, '77).

" . . . and the powers of death shall never conquer it." (NEB, '76).

Not one of these eight versions uses the word "Hell," substituting instead, "death," "netherworld," "underworld," or "Hades"; whereas, the *Douay-Rheims Bible* uses "Hell" without shame or apology. If a translation does not call Hell "Hell," *how are people supposed to know the Bible is saying* **"Hell"?**

The Latin Vulgate reads as follows: " . . . *ét* (and) *portae* (gates) *inferi* (of the lower world, or Hell) *non* (not) *praevalebunt* (shall prevail) *adversus* (against) *eam* (it)." In Greek it reads: " . . . *kaì* (and) *púlai* (the gates) *hádou* (of Hell, Hades) *oủ* (not) *katischúsousin* (shall prevail against) *aủtẽs* (it)."

The question in this passage comes down to how to translate correctly the Greek word *hádou* (which means, "Hell" or Hades) and the Latin *inferi* ("of the lower world," or "Hell"). Obviously, it is wrong to translate these two words as "death," for in Greek the word for death is *thánatos*, and in Latin *mors, mortis* ("death"). It is also incorrect to use the word "Hades," which depicts the state to which the souls of the dead go in the conception of the Greeks and Romans **of the pre-Christian era**; and "Hades" is definitely not an equivalent to the Christian concept of Hell, which entails a state of everlasting damnation, separation from God forever, an unquenchable fire, and unimaginable torment at the hands of the devils.

Hades, the underworld, the netherworld, on the other hand, represent a state of general sorrow and sadness at not being alive and at being separated from one's loved ones in the world. The idea of Hades was indistinct in the minds of the pre-Christian (non-Israelite) ancients, who had not yet received the revelation of Christ.

The Christian concept of Hell and the pre-Christian concept of Hades are vastly different indeed, and whereas the Greek and Latin **words** for our Christian notion of Hell are the same as those which represent the pre-Christian conception of the afterlife in the lower world, their translation has to be taken in the Christian conception of **Hell**, because they appear in the Christian, divinely inspired Scripture. "*Hádes* (Vulg. *infernus*) in the New Testament always designates the Hell of the damned." ("Hell," *Cath. Encyclopedia,* 1910, Vol. VII, p. 207). Therefore, the only way to translate these words from the Greek original and from the Latin is by the English word "Hell." **It is Hell they refer to and it is "Hell" they should be called!**

It is a dreadful mistake and a terrible disservice for modern translators to use "underworld," "netherworld," or "Hades" to represent the Christian concept of Hell because Hades (etc.) is the meaning of the word for the pre-Christian ancient peoples. And it is a travesty to call it "death." "Netherworld" indeed! The Catholic notion of Hell reflected on even momentarily is sufficient to put the fear of God into just about anyone! "Netherworld" leaves one unmoved. And "the gates of hell shall not prevail against it" is an open prophecy that the devils will try their utmost to destroy Christ's Church, the vehicle of salvation for all mankind, but that they will fail. Yet all this understanding is gone from the modern translations of this passage. Any priest or bishop who can recommend these new "bibles," knowing this type of glaring error exists in them, will have to answer to Our

Lord for the souls he has thereby allowed to be deceived!

"How Shall This Be Done . . .?"

In *Luke* 1:34 we read, **"And Mary said to the angel: How shall this be done, because I know not man?"** (DRB).

"Shall be done" in Greek is *estai,* a simple future tense—the sentence reads: "*Põs* (How) *'éstai* (shall be done) *toũto* (this), *èpeì* (because) *'ándra* (man) *òú* (not) *ginósko* (I know)? St. Jerome in the *Latin Vulgate* translates it, "*Quomodo* (in what manner, how) *fiet* (shall be done) *istud* (this), *quoniam* (because) *virum* (man) *non* (not) *cognosco* (I know)." (In Biblical terminology, the verb "to know" can refer to the intimate relations between a man and a woman.)

Now watch what the modern linguistic magicians do:

"How can this be since I do not know man?" (NAB, '70).

"How can this be, since I have no relations with a man?" (NAB, '86).

"But how can this come about, since I am a virgin?" (JB, '66).

"How can this be, since I have no husband?" (CRSV, '66). (Consider the absolute silliness of this version—especially today, when the illegitimacy rate in the U.S. is over fifty percent.)

Now let us consider the five Protestant renderings:

"How can this be, since I am a virgin?" (NASV, '77).

"'How will this be,' Mary asked the Angel, 'since I am a virgin?'" (NIV, '78).

"How can this be, since I am a virgin?" (NRSV, '89).

"How can this be, since I do not know a man?" (NKJV, '85).

"'How can this be?' said Mary; 'I am *still* a virgin.'" (NEB, '76, emphasis added).

Notice that changing "How shall this be done" to "How **can** this be" makes Mary appear to doubt the Angel's words as did Zachary when told that his wife would bear a son in her old age. (*Luke* 1:5-20). In fact, Scripture later records that St. Elizabeth praised Our Lady precisely because she *did* believe the Angel: "And blessed art thou that hast believed, because those things shall be accomplished that were spoken to thee by the Lord." (*Luke* 1:45, DRB). Also note that in the "original" Greek no mention is made about Mary's being a virgin, let alone, "*still* a virgin." The "original" Greek simply says, "I know not man," which *means* that she is a virgin and can imply that she plans to remain such.

This verse is another example of pure invention on the part of the translators; introducing "can" for "shall" alters the entire tone of the verse. But the most amazing aspect is that these new translations all ape one another in their error of introducing the word "can" with nothing in the original Greek to warrant their deviation from what Scripture actually says here (not to mention their adding the words "virgin," "still a virgin," etc.). Their contrivances are an insult to a person's intelligence and a blasphemy against Almighty God in His Revealed Word. **(After all, it is *His* Word, not theirs!)** The New English Bible would go so far as to imply that Mary planned some day to marry and have children; whereas, our Catholic Traditions say that she had already made a vow of virginity, and *official* Catholic Tradition teaches that she did in fact remain a virgin all her life. What will become of our

Catholic traditions if they are implicitly contradicted by the very Bible translations authorized by our bishops, for who would know that these new renderings are often only *approximate* "translations," save one familiar with the original language?

Judas' Betrayal

Let us now consider a brief passage from the arrest of Jesus. When Judas and the crowd came to apprehend Jesus in the Garden of Gethsemane, Jesus asked Judas a question, as recorded in *Matthew* 26:50. In the *Catholic Revised Standard Version* it reads, "Friend, why are you here?" (CRSV, '66). In the *New King James Version* it goes, "Friend, why have you come?" (NKJV, '85).

But in the *Vulgate* it is simply: "*Amice* (Friend), *ad* (to) *quid* (what) *venisti* (have you come)?" In Greek it reads, "'*Hetaîre* (Companion, Friend), *èph'* (to) hò (what) *párei* (are you come)?" '*Eph* is a form of *èpì*, used here with the accusative case (a direct object); *èpì* with the accusative has a dual meaning. It can mean "to a place or state" ("To what have you come?"), or "for a purpose" ("What have you come for?"). Both the *Latin Vulgate* and the *Douay-Rheims Bible* preserve this subtle ambiguity of the Greek, leaving the symbolic meaning *also* still present—as one can well imagine the infinite intelligence of Our Lord instilling into this question. But the other new Catholic translations and the NIV, NRSV and NASV make this verse into an imperative sentence.

"Friend, do what you are here for!" (NAB, '70).

"Friend, do what you have come for. (NAB, '86).

"My Friend, do what you are here for." (JB, '66).

"Friend, do what you came for." (NIV, '78).

"Friend, do what you are here to do." (NRSV, '89).

"Friend, *do* what you have come for." (NASV, '77).

"Friend, do what you are here to do." (NEB, '76).

Not a one of these "translations" is rendering what Scripture says! They are all rewording this verse into either a prosaic question or an imperative sentence that commands Judas to do what he came for. One has to ask, "Where did they get these contrivances?" They are not in the *Latin Vulgate*, and they are definitely not in the Greek "original." We are not considering here Hebrew or Chaldaic, over which some arcane argument might be introduced, but Greek, a language commonly taught in most universities.

But now listen to the *Douay-Rheims Bible:* **"Friend, whereto art thou come?" (DRB).** This is a two-pronged question, just as in the Greek and Latin: "Why are you here?" and "To what a state have you come?" Considered in the second sense, what is this question if not a moral rebuke leveled at Judas, which says in effect, "Friend, to what a state have you fallen to betray Me, the Son of Man, your God and Redeemer?" "How *low* have you descended to be able to do this to your God?"

But Our Lord can also ask the very same question of anyone who commits a sin and thereby betrays Him. Therefore, **this is a question asked, not just of Judas, but of us all! To what a state, indeed, do we descend to betray the Son of God by our sins, by our moral rebellion?** A person can pause here to meditate long and fruitfully on these five simple words from the *Douay-Rheims*. But in all the other versions, they become only part of a narrative—nothing to contemplate, nothing over which to call ourselves to task. No, just . . . on with the story, for more and more bland narrative!

Whereas, in the *Douay-Rheims Bible*, Our Lord utters a short, verbal stab that goes right to the heart of every sinner—something that can be said to him about every sin he commits—mortal or venial! For all sins are a betrayal of Christ, of His Person, of His Law, of His love. Every sin is a lie; it is also an idol—a false god—that we sinners place before the one, true God. In sum, it is a rejection and a betrayal of Him—plus that which caused His bitter agony and death. All this meaning from five simple words of Scripture . . . but Scripture faithfully translated!

"Peace on Earth . . ."

One of the most interesting examples to demonstrate how the modern translators often differ from St. Jerome's *Latin Vulgate Bible* occurs in *Luke* 2:14, where the Angels at the birth of Jesus are singing in their praise:

"Glory to God in the highest; and on earth, peace to men of good will." (DRB).

The ways this verse is translated in the various modern versions contain two examples of typical problems the translators face when they depart from St. Jerome's *Latin Vulgate Bible*. The **first** of these problems is exemplified by the translation of this verse in the original King James Version of 1611, which translation is then repeated by the NKJV, seemingly because this verse the way the KJV rendered it is so famous. In both the KJV and NKJV it reads:

"Glory to God in the highest, and on earth **peace, good will toward men."** (KJV and NKJV, emphasis added).

This translation conveys a fundamentally different concept from that of the DRB and *Latin Vulgate*. The KJV and NKJV imply that there is now "an open divine accord and peace with mankind," whereas the DRB, reflecting the *Latin Vulgate* of St. Jerome, says, "peace to men **of good will**"—with the implication of **only** "to men of good will."

Which is right? How did the King James

Commission arrive at this translation? (And is that sufficient reason for the NKJV to retain it?) For the NKJV is the *only* version that does retain this translation among the 10 versions compared here. (St. Jerome in his *Latin Vulgate* obviously does not agree with this translation either.)

To answer these two questions, let us first consider the *Latin Vulgate* translation and then the edition of the "original" Greek available to us today:

In Latin, the words are verbatim the same as in the DRB: "*Gloria* (Glory) *in* (in) *altissimis* (the highest) *Deo* (to God), *et* (and) *in* (on) *terra* (earth) *pax* (peace) *hominibus* (to men) *bonae* (of good) *voluntatis* (will)."

And in the Greek, they are again word for word the same: "*Dóxa* (Glory) *èn* (in) *hupsístois* (the highest) *Theó* (to God) *kaì* (and) *èpì* (on) *gẽs* (earth) *èiréne* (peace) *'en* (to) *'anthrópois* (men) *eủdokías* (of good will)." (Cf. Liddell-Scott, *eủdokía,* p. 324.)

The difference in translation in the KJV and NKJV from the DRB and all other modern translations cited here, plus in the *Latin Vulgate*, comes down to the **"case"** of the Greek word *eủdokías,* which is a possessive (i.e., genitive) case form, as given here. But some Greek texts have *eὐdokías* as *eὐdokía,* which is a nominative case form, i.e., the case of the subject of a sentence. The KJV and NKJV are based on this other Greek version. Therefore, the KJV and NKJV are considering *eὐdokía* either an appositive of the subject of the sentence (i.e., a repeat), or the second half of a compound subject: ". . . peace, good will toward men." The DRB translates *eὐdokías* as "**of** good will," which is how St. Jerome translates it (*bonae voluntatis*).

However, one should note well that both the KJV and NKJV translate *eὐdokías* (i.e., *eὐdokía* to them) as "*good will.*" This agrees with the DRB, but it is in contradistinction to all the other modern translations compared here, other than the DRB. (This is an important point which we shall discuss later in this section.)

This discrepancy in the Greek text is an example of the reason the Douay-Rheims Bible translators adopted a policy of trusting St. Jerome's Latin Vulgate over the Greek versions when there occurs a difference in the ancient texts, because in their words, the Vulgate is "more pure then the Hebrew or Greeke now extant" and "the same Latin hath bene farre better conserved from corruptions." (Preface to the *Douay Old Testament*). (This greater fidelity in the *Vulgate* was due in large part to there being far more copies made of the *Vulgate* than of the Greek and Hebrew bibles.)

Here, it seems to this writer, we need to defer to St. Jerome and to trust in God's providence that the Greek text he translated from was correct and that he translated it correctly. From numerous passages in both the Old and New Testaments, for example, one can clearly see that God distinguishes between the "just" (the good, those "in the state of sanctifying grace") and the "unjust" (mortal sinners) in His relationship to human beings. He does not hold out *open* "good will" to mortal sinners, but dire warnings (and even threatened punishments) that they should change their ways. From this fact alone—i.e., the disagreement between the message of "peace, good will to men" (KJV, NKJV) and the warnings to and strictures against sinners in the rest of the Bible—it would seem far wiser to accept St. Jerome (and his wording of "peace to men of good will"), for he was Greek-speaking from birth, was closer than we to the writing of the New

Testament by (now) some 1,600 years, and had many manuscripts to work from that are no longer extant.

The point is not really hard; it comes down to this: trusting St. Jerome and the Holy Spirit—St. Jerome because he was Greek-speaking, a genius, a Saint (he translated on his knees in prayer and humility and was obviously singled out by God to do what he did) and the Holy Spirit because He allowed THIS translation to stand from 409 to 1611, before it was challenged by the Protestants with the KJV. One has to ask himself: "Were all those Catholic centuries lost in the darkness of ignorance about this Scripture passage until enlightened by the Protestants?" Or, did the Catholic Church have it right all along?

Now let us consider the **second** problem: what the other versions do with *eủdokías* ("of good will") in this verse.

Every other version in English cited here has something quite different from "of good will" that we find in the *Douay-Rheims*, the *Latin Vulgate*, and the Greek "original"—and even from the KJV and NKJV. Here are these modern translations:

"Glory to God in high heaven, peace on earth *to those on whom his favor rests.*" (NAB, '70, emphasis added).

"Glory to God in the highest, and on earth *peace to those on whom his favor rests.*" (NAB, '86, emphasis added).

"Glory to God in the highest heaven, and *peace to men who enjoy his favour.*" (JB, '66, emphasis added).

"Glory to God in the highest, and on earth *peace among men with whom he is pleased.*" (CRSV, '66 and NASV, '77, emphasis added).

"Glory to God in the highest heaven, and on earth *peace among those whom he favors!*" (NRSV, '89, emphasis added).

"Glory to God in the highest, and on earth *peace to men on whom his favor rests.*" (NIV, '78, emphasis added).

"Glory to God in highest heaven, and on earth his *peace for men on whom his favor rests.*" (NEB, '76, emphasis added).

What leads to the wide disparity among translations of this passage between the DRB on the one hand and all these others is that **the Greek noun *eủdokía(s)* is just plain hard to translate**. The *Greek-English Lexicon* by Liddell-Scott gives two meanings for *eủdokía*: "satisfaction" or "approval." However, neither one of these fits the context of the sentence, nor do they agree with the *Latin Vulgate*, the *Douay-Rheims Bible*, or even the King James Versions. To translate the verse ". . . peace to men of satisfaction" or ". . . peace to men of approval" would be stupid, so the modern translators did not do this. It is the opinion of this writer that they were stumped, that the correct English translation for the word as used in this passage simply is not found in today's Greek-English lexicons, and therefore, as an intelligent way out of their problem, they would seem to have gone to those famous passages in the New Testament where God the Father, at Jesus' baptism and transfiguration, says, "This is my beloved Son, in whom I am well pleased" (*Matt.* 3:17, and *Matt.* 17:5, DRB), plus other similar passages, and built up a meaning out of the verb form of *eủdokías*—which they knew the meaning of.

The Greek form of the verb for "am well pleased" is *eủdókesa,* which is very similar in form to the noun *eủdokía.* Thus, in the opinion of this writer, they improvised translations such as ". . . on whom his favor rests" (NAB, '70 and '86, NIV, '78 and NEB

'76), ". . . who enjoy his favor" (JB, '66), ". . . with whom he is pleased" (CRSV and NASV), and ". . . among those whom he favors" (NRSV, '89).

One has to admit that this is very ingenious of the translators because they can thereby render an approximate meaning that fits the context of the sentence, the general meaning of the *Vulgate* and the traditional English of the DRB. There is only one problem, however: **This is not what the Bible says—not in the Greek text nor in the *Vulgate!*** These modern versions are putting words into the mouth of St. Matthew—and in turn, of Almighty God, who inspired the Scriptures—words that are just not there and in turn that are changing the meaning of the verse. (Notice, e.g., that "peace on earth" is entirely gone from the JB.)

What does the Greek say? ". . . *kaì* (and) *ѐpi* (on) *gẽs* (earth) *'eiréne* (peace) *ѐn* (to) *anthrópois* (men) *eủdokías* ('of good' *something or other*)" . . . **"will,"** according to St. Jerome, but definitely not "satisfaction" or "approval," as Liddell-Scott gives the translation). We know that *eủdokías* is the possessive form of the noun and that the Greek prefix *eủ-* means "good" or "well."

(We still use this prefix in English, as in "eulogy," "eugenics," "euphemism," etc.) Therefore we know two of the three components of *eὐdokías,* namely, "of" and "good." It comes down to this, then: what does the *-dokías* part mean?

The answer is really not very hard: We just need to accept St. Jerome's rendering—"of good will." The KJV did—at least the "good will" part. What is the *problem* with accepting St. Jerome? It is the opinion of this writer that today's Greek lexicons and dictionaries have lost the "good will" meaning of *eὐdokía*; probably it was a 4th or 5th meaning of the noun, or maybe a 10th or 12th, and its meaning has been lost to the scholars who have had to assemble their mighty, brilliant lexicons from the many usages of the words found in all of ancient literature. But did they capture for posterity **all** the meanings in **all** the passages? This would seem hardly likely! Only an army of scholars in our own time, using a capacious computer system, could even *approach* this objective . . . and that only after many years of work.

The reader will perhaps forebear a homely, first-hand example to illustrate the point: Recently in this writer's office, he used a common word no one had ever heard used that way. The unabridged *Webster's Dictionary* gave this usage as the **13th meaning of the word**. Sixteen hundred years from now, will scholars still know this 13th meaning of that word? Probably not! The correct meaning of *eủdokías* is probably in that same situation vis-a-vis the modern translators. But if it is a bona fide 4th or 6th or 8th or 10th meaning of the word, do you suppose the Greek St. Jerome knew it? The safer bet is that he did. Just look at what he did with it: "of good will" is simple, straight-forward and intelligible; also, it fits—not just linguistically, but with the entire theology of the Bible! Plus, it has lasted 16 centuries really unchallenged, even by the original KJV. (The King James Commission also called it "good will.") Should not modern scholars then also accept it today—trusting that in the mind of that ancient Greek Saint the precise meaning of *eủdokías* was surely and safely stored away, so that, in God's providence, he could give it to us?

Then too, let us consider that the intellectuals of St. Jerome's day throughout the Roman Empire all knew Greek and Latin, and **they** all accepted his translation. If the whole Greco-Roman intellectual world accepted it, why do modern translators have a problem with it? What is afoot here? Are the modern translators uncircumspect as to ask us to accept *their* contrived translation—because their lexicons do not translate *eủdokías* as "of good will" (*bonae voluntatis*)—when the whole Greek-and-Latin-speaking ancient world did accept it? Which side has the greater probability for accuracy? If a person's life depended on the choice, there is not a doubt which way he would decide. (In this writer's experience, learned people can often get bollixed up by not carefully thinking through all the implications of what they are doing or writing when it flies in the face of tradition.)

The *Latin Vulgate* definitely does not say, "peace, good will toward men," as the KJV and NKJV version would have it, implying thereby an equal good will to "*all* men." St. Paul, before his conversion, was truly a man on whom God's favor rested, but can we believe that, *while he was persecuting the Church*, God would wish him "peace," rather than a very disturbed conscience, until such time as he would become "of good will"? (Christ knocked him off his horse and temporarily blinded him to wake him up!) There is truly a difference between "God's favor" on the one hand and "good will" in one's heart on the other. Are we to imagine that the Angels, with their pure, untrammeled intellects, did not see the truth in such an elementary matter?

And how the NAB can go so far as *not* to translate *ánthropois* as "men" displays a freedom with the text that simply fails to respect what the Bible says. Every adult can see that our word "anthropology," "the study of man," comes etymologically from the Greek word *anthropos,* "man." Granted the translators of the NAB may want to use terms "inclusive" of men *and* women, yet clearly that is *not* what Scripture says.

A translation that takes such liberties is truly only an *approximation* of what the Bible actually says. And yet it is the NAB that outsells all other Catholic Bibles combined, because the clergy and teachers promote it. Also, it is the version usually used in the new Catholic liturgy in English in the U.S. It is the version most Catholic school children are sent off to procure. But what if a person were to attempt to do St. Ignatius' *Spiritual Exercises* using the *New American Bible*; would he ever arrive at a penetration of what the Bible really means, or would he derive only some vague approximation of the meaning—if even that?

Are we to discard the time-honored use of "man" and "men" to refer in a generic sense to all mankind, now that the fad of modern feminism has been foisted on the world—as if Jesus Christ did not truly liberate women 2000 years ago and raise them to a dignity in many ways superior to man's . . . from which current women's liberation has only dragged them down?

"What Does It Profit . . .?"

In *Matthew* 16:26 there occurs one of the most arresting and sobering statements ever uttered by Our Lord—one that, in a single verse, casts man's entire existence on this earth into stark and clear perspective. He said: **"For what does it profit a man, if he gain the whole world, and suffer the loss of his own soul? Or what exchange shall a man give for his soul?" (DRB).**

In Latin this passage reads: "*Quid* (What) *enim* (for) *prodest* (does it profit) *homini* (a man), *si* (if) *mundum* (the world) *universum* (entire) *lucretur* (he gain), *animae* (of soul) *vero* (but) *suae* (his own) *detrimentum* (loss) *patiatur* (he suffer)? *Aut* (Or) *quam* (what) *dabit* (shall he give) *homo* (a man) *commutationen* (in exchange) *pro* (for) *anima* (soul) *sua* (his)?"

In Greek it reads: "*Tí* (What) *gàr* (for) *ȍphelēthḗsetai* (does it profit) *'ánthropos* (a man) *èàn* (if) *tón* (the) *kósmon* (world) *hólon* (whole) kerdḗsé (he gain), *tèn* (the) *dè* (but) *psuchèn* (soul) *aùtoũ* (of himself) *zēmiōthẽ* (suffers the loss of)? *Ḗ* (Or) *tí* (what) *dṓsei* (shall give) *'ánthropos* (a man) *'antállagma* (as exchange for) *tãs* (the) *psuchãs* (soul) *aủtoũ* (of himself)?

Now consider what the new Catholic bibles do with this gem:

"What profit would a man show if he were to gain the whole world and destroy himself in the process? What can a man offer in exchange for his very self?" (NAB, '70).

"What profit would there be for one to gain the whole world and forfeit his *life*? Or what can one give in exchange for his *life*?" (NAB, '86—emphasis added).

"For what will it profit a man if he gains the whole world and forfeits his *life*? Or what shall a man give in return for his *life*?" (CRSV, '66—emphasis added).

"What then will a man gain if he wins the whole world and ruins his *life*? Or what has a man to offer in exchange for his *life*?" (JB '66—emphasis added).

Now consider the Protestant versions:

"For what will it profit *them* if they gain the whole world but forfeit *their life?* Or what will they give in return for *their life?*" (NRSV, '89, emphasis added). (The translators of the NRSV do not even use the singular in this version, substituting "they" for "he".)

"What will a man gain by winning the whole world, at the cost of his true self? Or what can he give that will buy that self back?" (NEB, '76).

"For what is a man profited if he gains the whole world, and loses his own soul? Or what will a man give in exchange for his soul?" (NKJV, '85).

"What good will it be for a man if he gains the whole world, yet forfeits his soul? Or what can a man give in exchange for his soul?" (NIV, '78).

"For what will a man be profited, if he gains the whole world, and forfeits his soul? Or what will a man give in exchange for his soul?" (NASV, '77).

It is very interesting that three of the Protestant versions cited here (NKJV, NIV and NASV) all translate this passage basically correctly, but the three Catholic versions and the NRSV and NEB all get it dead wrong! The Greek word for "life" is *bios*, but for "soul," it is *psýche* (pronounced "psuchay"). From *bios* we get biology, biography, biosphere, etc. From *psýche* we derive psychology, psychosis, psychic, etc. The first means "life"; the second means "soul." No one has to study Greek to understand this; he just has to go to a basic English dictionary! The etymology is right there. As a professor-friend has commented on this passage:

"What these 'translators' are doing is pretending to know Hebrew better than the Evangelists. If Jesus was speaking Hebrew or Aramaic, he used *nephesh* or *naphshā*. These words do mean either 'soul' or 'life.' The Evangelist picked the 'soul' meaning when he translated the Lord's saying into Greek. Why assume that he picked the wrong meaning? Wasn't he inspired? Moreover, picking the 'life' meaning gives the saying a *morally false* meaning . . ."

What the modern Catholic translators (and those of the NRSV and NEB) have done with this passage is simply *lie* to people. **This passage is not mistranslated; it is forged!** And the forgery needs to be exposed. People need to take these Catholic "bibles" back to where they bought them and demand a refund. It is unconscionable for the Catholic clergy and hierarchy—if they know these things—to recommend any of these so-called Catholic "bibles" when they betray the very words of Our Lord with a patent, outright lie. In the new Catholic versions, this verse orients man to the world, to self-preservation—at any cost! In the *Douay-Rheims*, in the *Latin Vulgate*, in the "original" Greek, this verse orients a person toward Heaven, no matter what!

(Oh yes, the word *psýche* is onomatopoetic—sounds like its meaning—and in its ancient use represented "breath," which in turn represented "life," and therefore "soul," for when the breath goes out of a person at death ("psoooochaaaay"), the life of man has gone out along with his soul. But what student or even well-educated adult is going to see the remote, antiquarian, etymological connection of these two concepts? At the time the New Testament was written, the Greek word *psýche* had achieved, after many hundreds of years, the specific meaning "SOUL"! The translators have simply lied to their readers in this case!

From this and other evidence presented here, it would appear that these modern translators have a preconceived set of ideas (or even an agenda), and they are translating their ideas into the bibles they are producing—this despite what the "original" Greek says, and clearly means. It would seem that if no one calls their number, they will just go on deceiving!

"Power To Be Made The Sons of God"

In St. John's Gospel, Chapter 1, Verses 9 to 12, we read the following:

"That was the true light, which enlighteneth every man that cometh into this world. He was in the world, and the world was made by him, and the world knew him not. He came unto his own, and his own received him not. **But as many as received him, he gave them power *to be made the sons of God*,** to them that believe in his name." **(DRB)**. (*John* 1:9-12, emphasis added).

This last emphasized verse of St. John contains in a pithy microcosm the entire theology of grace for the conversion of sinners. For actually, man does very little in his own conversion; it is mostly God's (actual) grace at work to bring man to justification. (The reader should note that "justification" equals "conversion," which equals "receiving Sanctifying Grace," which equals "becoming an adopted child of God"—all of which takes place at Baptism.) Hear what the Council of Trent says, in this regard:

> It is furthermore declared that in adults the beginning of that justification must proceed from the predisposing grace of God through Jesus Christ, that is, from His vocation, whereby, without any merits on their part, they are called; that they who by sin had been cut off from God, may be disposed through His quickening and helping grace to convert themselves to their own justification *by freely assenting to and cooperating with that grace*; so that, while God touches the heart of

> man through the illumination of the Holy Ghost, man himself neither does absolutely nothing while receiving that inspiration, since he can also reject it, *nor yet is he able by his own free will and without the grace of God to move himself to justice in His sight*. Hence, when it is said in the Sacred Writings: "*Turn ye to me,. . . and I will turn to you*" [*Zacharias* 1:3], we are reminded of our liberty; and when we reply: "*Convert us, O Lord, to thee, and we shall be converted*" [*Lamentations* 5:21], we confess that we need the grace of God. (*Canons and Decrees of the Council of Trent*, 6th Sess., Chapter V, "Justification." Emphasis added.)

The Council of Trent goes on to say that in performing a grace-filled act, the will of man is free to accept or reject God's prevenient grace, which, if he accepts it, then moves him to accept Baptism.

Now listen again to the 12th Verse of *John* 1: "**But as many as received him, he gave them *power to be made* the**

sons of God, to them that believe in his name." (Emphasis added).

The Latin Vulgate reads: "*Quotquot* (as many as) *autem* (But) *receperunt* (they received) *eum* (Him), *dedit* (He gave) *eis* (to them) *potestatem* (the power) *filios* (the sons) *Dei* (of God) *fieri* (to be made)." And this translation is literally the same as the Greek "original."

The Greek "original" reads: "*Hosoi* (As many as) *dè* (but) *'élabon* (received) *'auton* (Him) *'édōken* (he gave) *'autoîs* (to them) *'exousían* (power) *tékna* (sons) *Theoũ* (of God) *genésthai* (to be made)."

But hear now how the new Catholic Bibles and the Protestant Bibles translate this verse:

"Any who did accept him *he empowered to become* children of God." (NAB, '70, emphasis added).

"But to those who did accept him *he gave power to become* children of God." (NAB, '86, emphasis added).

"But to all who received him, who believed in his name, *he gave power to become* children of God." (CRSV, '66, emphasis added).

"But to all who did accept him *he gave*

power to become children of God." (JB, '66, emphasis added).

"But as many as received Him, to them *He gave the right to become* children of God." (NKJV, '85, emphasis added).

"Yet to all who received him, to those who believed in his name, *he gave the right to become* children of God." (NIV, '78, emphasis added).

"But as many as received Him, to them *He gave the right to become* children of God." (NASV, '77, emphasis added).

"But to all who received him, who believed in his name, *he gave power to become* children of God." (NRSV, '89, emphasis added).

"But to all who did receive him, to those who have yielded him their allegiance, *he gave the right to become* children of God." (NEB, '76, emphasis added).

Cassel's Latin-English and English-Latin Dictionary gives "to be made" as the literal translation of the Latin passive infinitive *fieri*, and only a remote meaning of "to become." And *genésthai* is the second aorist Greek infinitive of *gígnomai*, whose primary meaning is "to be made," which is always a passive infinitive, and in English is translated "to be made" (a passive infinitive). Yet **every one of the nine translations cited immediately above** translates *fieri* and *genésthai* as "to become." Only the *Douay-Rheims* says "to be made," which is the primary, literal meaning of *fieri* and *genésthai*. Notice also that four Protestant versions (NKJV, NIV, NASV and NEB) translate the Greek *èxousían* and Latin *potestatem* ("the power") as "the right," another gratuitous, "creative" translation.

Some may argue that this discussion appears to be "straining out the gnat." However, just the opposite is the case: far from being trivial, the poor translation of this passage from *John* 1:12 in all the non-*Douay-Rheims* versions shows, it would seem, both a certain arrogance toward the actual wording of the Bible, on the one hand, and on the other, an absence of regard for the precise theology of grace that St. John is expressing in this verse.

Both the Greek word *genésthai* and the Latin word *fieri* are passive infinitives, which mean precisely, "to be made." Now the *Douay-Rheims Bible* translates these two passive infinitives with the English passive infinitive "to be made." The exact meaning of the Greek "original" and the Latin Vulgate translation thereof are retained perfectly by the *Douay-Rheims*. However, this verse is skewed by every other English version cited here. All nine of these popular English translations use an **active infinitive** ("to become"), rather than the passive infinitive ("to be made"), which is used by the original Greek, as if we could—after Christ's initial help—**change ourselves** into children of God!

Granted, "he gave them **power to be made** the sons of God" (DRB) at first sight does not seem to make sense. Rather, it appears to be a self-contradictory statement. Presumably, that is why all the other popular modern English translations cited here say "power [or right] **to become**." At first glance, they would appear to be correct—from the easy flow of the English sentence. However, two powerful objections to this translation ("to become") can be made.

First of all, **it is not what Scripture says**! And secondly, **it opens the door to the Pelagian heresy** (5th century), or at least to the Semipelagian heresy (which was condemned by the Second Council of Orange in 529). Pelagianism, among other teachings, held that *by nature* man can perform good works that merit salvation, *without* the grace of God; that the role of Christ is *only* that of "example" or "instruction," which man freely accepts; that the prompting of God's grace is not necessary, either for the *beginning* or the *accomplishment* of a meritorious act; and that man chooses virtue by his own natural power. Semipelagianism held that grace is necessary for the *accomplishment* of good works, but not for their *initiation* or beginning, which man initially chooses by his free will unaided by God's grace.

Now these are the very errors that the Protestants of the 16th century accused the Catholic Church of having fallen into. However, the correct and Catholic teaching on divine grace and justification says that God prompts man by His divine assistance (grace) not only to **commence** but also to **accomplish** (or finish) virtuous acts and that man responds by co-operating with God's promptings of grace by means of his free will. God sustains man at every step of the process of justification; He does not hand over to us "the power to become sons of God," as the inaccurate modern translations state it.

Again, we cite part of the dogmatic definition of the Council of Trent:

> . . .while God touches the heart of man through the illumination of the Holy Ghost, man himself neither does absolutely nothing while receiving that inspiration, since he can also reject it, *nor yet is he able by his own free will and without the grace of God to move himself to justice in His sight.* (*Canons and Decrees of the Council of Trent,* 6th Sess., Chapter V, Justification. Emphasis added.)

In contrast to this balanced doctrine, the Protestant teaching that man contributes nothing to his justification led to the determinism of John Calvin (1509-1564) and to the false Calvinistic teaching on predestination. Man's free will was thereby denied.

But, the inaccurate translation of *John* 1:12 opens the door to the idea that man's free will is sufficient by itself to perform acts meritorious of salvation (the condemned heresy of Pelagianism or Semipelagianism). Therefore, whereas the correct translation in the *Douay-Rheims*

Bible—"he gave them **power to be made** the sons of God"—appears at first sight to be self-contradictory, it in fact reveals the precise truth of how justification occurs: i.e., God initiates it by the promptings of His prevenient grace (that grace which "goes before"), plus helps man to accomplish it by the on-going promptings of His continuing grace, all the way through the act. The role of man's free will is to accept and respond to God's grace . . . or to reject it. To repeat: God sustains man at every step of the process of justification; He does not hand over to us "the power **to become** sons of God," as the inaccurate modern translations state it.

The manner in which God's grace works, in co-operation with man's free will is admitted by all theologians to be the most difficult part of theology. It is understandable, then, why the **correct** translation of *John* 1:12 would appear at first to be so difficult as to be unintelligible and therefore presumably wrong. But that is not a reason to adapt Scripture by a smoother but inaccurate translation and thereby open the way to heresy.

One has to wonder how the many translators of these modern versions can so consistently agree to disagree from the original Scripture in this instance. Are they—in some effort to make the Bible read more simply—so arrogant as to disregard what the original Greek text actually says? Or are they ignorant of the Catholic theology of the grace of justification—expressed so perfectly here by St. John, and elsewhere by St. Paul?

Whatever may be the reason for their mistranslation, the exactitude and fidelity of the *Douay-Rheims Bible* to the Greek original of the New Testament is once more demonstrated by *John* 1:12. A person meditating on this passage of St. John will be awe-struck by the smallness of man's part in his own justification and the major, major role played by the grace of God—*i.e.*, by God, the Holy Spirit, acting on the soul. And such is exactly what our Catholic theology of the grace of justification teaches, as borne out in the passage cited from the Council of Trent.

"I Will Begin To Vomit Thee Out of My Mouth"

There exists in the *Apocalypse (Revelation)*, Chapter 3, Verses 15 and 16, one of the most powerful and frightening passages in all of Sacred Scripture. Our Lord here is speaking to the "angel of the church of Laodicea," i.e., to the bishop of that diocese. But His words have a general reference to all people, and during all times. He says: **"I know thy works, that thou art neither cold, nor hot. I would thou wert cold, or hot. But because thou art lukewarm, and neither cold, nor hot, I will begin to vomit thee out of my mouth." (DRB).**

The other versions are generally quite similar to each other in their translation of these verses, as well as to the *Douay-Rheims* translation, **except for two key words**: 1) "vomit"—*evomere* in Latin, meaning literally "to vomit forth"; and *èmésai* in Greek, translated, again, literally and only, "to vomit"; plus, 2) "I will begin to"—*incipiam* in Latin, meaning literally, "I shall begin"; and *méllo* in Greek, meaning literally, "to be about to." However, translating these two words incorrectly makes all the difference in the world to the meaning of this incomparable passage.

Following is how the other versions translate these verses:

"I know your deeds; I know you are neither hot nor cold. How I wish you were one or the other—hot or cold! But because you are lukewarm, neither hot nor cold, I will *spew* you out of my mouth." (NAB, '70, emphasis added).

"I know your works; I know that you are neither cold nor hot. I wish you were either cold or hot. So, because you are lukewarm, neither hot nor cold, I will *spit* you out of my mouth." (NAB, '86, emphasis added).

"I know your works: you are neither cold nor hot. Would that you were cold or hot! So, because you are lukewarm and neither cold nor hot, I will *spew* you out of my mouth." (CRSV, '66, emphasis added).

"I know *all about you* [?]; how you are neither cold nor hot. I wish you were *one or the other* [?], but since you are neither, but only lukewarm, I will *spit* you out of my mouth." (JB, '66, emphasis added).

"I know your works, that you are neither cold nor hot. I *could wish* [?] you were cold or hot. So then, because you are lukewarm, and neither cold nor hot, I will *spew* you out of My mouth." (NKJV, '85, emphasis added).

"I know your *deeds* [?], that you are neither cold nor hot. I wish you were either one or the other! [?] So, because you are lukewarm—neither hot nor cold—I *am about to spit* you out of my mouth." (NIV, '78, emphasis added).

"I know your works; you are neither cold nor hot. I wish that you were either cold or hot. So, because you are lukewarm, and neither cold nor hot, *I am about to spit* you out of my mouth." (NRSV, '89, emphasis added).

"I know your *deeds* [?], that you are neither cold nor hot; I would that you were cold or hot. So because you are lukewarm, and neither hot nor cold, I will *spit* you out of My mouth." (NASV, '77, emphasis added).

"I know all your ways; you are neither hot nor cold. How I wish you were either hot or cold! But because you are lukewarm, neither hot nor cold, I will *spit* you out of my mouth." (NEB, '76, emphasis added).

The NIV and the *New American Standard Version* translate *opera*, "works" (in Greek, *erga*—"works"), as "deeds," not "works"; the NEB calls them "ways." The NAB, the JB, the NIV, the NASV and the NEB say "spit" for "vomit," and the others say "spew"; whereas, the word used is "vomit" (*evomere* in Latin and *èmésai* in

Greek). (The Greek verb ptúein means "to spit.") Our Lord says, "I will begin" (*méllo* in Greek and *incipiam* in Latin, both meaning literally, "I will begin") "to vomit" (*evomere* in Latin, "to vomit forth," and *èmésai* in Greek, "to vomit"). But the NAB, CRSV, JB, NKJV, and NASV all drop off the "I will begin"; only the NIV and the NRSV have this element, but nonetheless, they use "spit," rather than "vomit."

Now "to vomit" is a disgusting act, one of the *most* disgusting to human beings. It means to eject partially digested food from the stomach, from the inner part of a person. Christians are part of Christ's Mystical Body, part of His mystical inner being. To be vomited forth is to be rejected by Christ, to be ejected from Him. A person only vomits when he can no longer hold down the food that is upsetting his stomach. Rather than vomit, a person would a hundred times sooner settle his stomach and have the food digest. From this verse of Scripture we learn that the same is true of Christ relative to the lukewarm. He would seem to want to retain them, but simply cannot stomach them. And He is *about* to vomit them forth.

But one should notice the use of "I will

begin to," meaning that He has not done it *yet*, but is about to—sort of like the spontaneous action of vomiting. For vomiting is preceded by a certain period of nausea or upset before it occurs. During this time the sick person "is about to" vomit. Thus, this entire passage is *perfectly* suited to the subject and *is a warning to the lukewarm to change or else to be rejected by Christ.* **These subtleties are missed by all the versions**, except by the NIV and NRSV with regard to "I am about to." Yet **every single one of the nine non-*Douay-Rheims* versions fails to use the extremely powerful word "vomit,"** which is the *key* word to this entire passage, giving it the power and character that make it one of Scripture's most striking and memorable statements.

Most of us, after all, *are* lukewarm, or *tend* toward lukewarmness, and are neither cold nor hot in our relation to Christ. From these verses we see starkly that this quality of our lukewarm affection for Christ is so revolting to Him that He cannot assimilate (digest) us into His Mystical Body, and He is so "upset" by our attitude that He will *begin* to "vomit" us out of His mouth.

A little meditative reflection on the symbolism of this passage yields results rich in meaning—if the passage is correctly translated. But "spit" and "spew" give nothing near the same meaning as "vomit." "I will spit [or 'spew'] you out of my mouth" leaves **no hope** for the lukewarm; whereas, "I will begin to" and "vomit" actually leave **some hope** that a person, by changing, can repent, can amend his life and become agreeable and acceptable to Christ and thus can remain within His Mystical Body. The image used in these verses is profound and perfect; it is ripe with meaning—*if* the verses are properly translated!

Considering, only this one passage, a person can see most graphically how the *Douay-Rheims Bible* is filled with life, while the other translations are relatively dead and time and again simply mistranslate the Bible. All this power, all these fine distinctions and meanings come from just a few common words of Scripture . . . but from a few words properly translated!

Conclusion

Many other examples could be brought forward to buttress the conclusion of this writer that the four modern Catholic Bibles in English reviewed here are simply not literally accurate and therefore are not trustworthy; plus, that the Protestant translations reviewed are not much better. They are not careful, word-for-word translations of Scripture, but rather, and at best, somewhat loose, colloquial *"approximations"* of the meaning of the Bible—in many instances as filtered through the minds of the translators.

The point, of course, is this: What translator—or translators taken even collectively—can possibly outguess God on all the meanings He has inspired into the text of Scripture? When a person reads slowly and carefully the one literal and accurate English translation of the Bible, the *Douay-Rheims*, and especially if he will *meditate* on the passages, he can pick up these subtle meanings. And often these meanings contain the clues and the answers to the very problems he has been seeking to solve.

Consider also the priest in preparing his sermons: If he has meditated deeply upon various Scriptural passages—after the manner of St. Ignatius' *Spiritual Exercises*—then he will be like the "scribe instructed in the kingdom of heaven" mentioned by Our Lord, who "is like to a man that is a householder, who bringeth forth out of his treasure new things and old." (*Matt.* 13:52). In other words, his study and meditation on Scripture and the Divine Revelation of God gives him a "treasure" to use in preaching and in instruction, because he has carefully probed Scripture and has plumbed many of the profound meanings secreted there by Almighty God. But if these meanings have been inadvertently (or purposely) translated out of the text, because the translators are using wrong methods of translating, how are we, or how is that priest, even to suspect those meanings were there to begin with? Especially will the priest be crippled in his work as teacher and preacher if the subtle and profound meanings implanted in the Sacred Text under the inspiration of the Holy Ghost have been translated away, for the priests leads the flock and most priests today do not study Latin and Greek, as they formerly were required to do.

The million-dollar question is this: How did all this happen? How have these modern translators gotten away with their bogus translations for so long? Why have not the priests and bishops said something long 'ere this?

The explanation of *how it happened* was given earlier: The translators of the modern Catholic bibles, according to the thesis of this little book, make three errors: 1) **they trust texts other than St. Jerome's *Vulgate***, texts that are not so reliable as his in every instance; 2) they employ **translations** of certain words that are true meanings of the words, but meanings **that do not always fit the use employed in the particular passages of the Bible in question** and/or are not the traditional meanings; and 3) they often fall into the error of **translating their *understanding* of the meaning of the Bible**, instead of what the Bible actually says.

Our priests and bishops, by and large, are extremely busy men and have little time for close research into such a technical matter as biblical study—a study, moreover, that requires expertise in Hebrew, Greek and Latin. How many of us can come to competence in even modern French, Spanish or German, let alone in three dead languages, and that to a degree sufficient to dispute with the "authorities"?

It would appear that, in the interest of having a newer version of Scripture, the hierarchy accepted what was given them as "newer" without having been prepared to examine carefully the revolutionary texts they were given. Archbishop Dwyer of Portland, Oregon claimed, for example, that the bishops were not even consulted on which version of Scripture would be employed when the New Mass was first introduced in the late 1960's. It was presented as an accomplished fact, with the "salve" that the translation was "only experimental" and would be improved.

The New Testament has now been totally redone, as of 1986, but one can see from the few examples cited here that the changes were minor and not enough! The Old Testament is currently also *being "improved"* and is due out in 2003. *Will they get it right this time?* It does not look too prospective, based on what we have seen they did with the "new" *New American* New Testament.

Are we going to trust these translators with another try . . . especially when so much is at stake? For while they have been bungling away, what sort of tragedy has been worked in the minds and lives and, yes, undoubtedly, in the eternal destiny of the many poor souls who have been misguidedly studying these corrupted Bible translations? And what about young people, who by and large have no idea that there is any problem with what they read in these modern bibles? Is it not high time that an end were put to this on-going disaster and that we return to the one truly safe and accurate translation of Scripture in English, namely, the *Douay-Rheims Bible*?

From just the little evidence brought forth in this tract, it is obvious that these many wrong translations should simply be scrapped, and the sooner the better. Without injuring anyone's faith, we could easily return to the *Douay-Rheims* version of Scripture. It is, after all, English—and quite excellent English at that. In fact, the newer translations are steadily coming closer and closer to the *Douay-Rheims* in many verses; and the closer they come, the more accurate they become. (All these modern translators really need to do to create a truly excellent English bible is to use the *Douay-Rheims* as a trot.) We take for granted that high school students will read Shakespeare (1564-1616). Why in the world cannot the rest of us be expected to read Challoner's *Douay-Rheims* (1749-1750), updated by Bishop Kenrick (1859)—especially when the salvation of our souls is at stake?

"But the *Douay-Rheims* is hard!" it will

be objected. "People can't understand it. The new Catholic versions at least enable many people to read the Bible who otherwise could not."

This entire line of argument is false: It is not the *Douay-Rheims* that is hard. *It is the Holy Bible that is hard!* As a Scripture professor-friend exclaimed to this writer: "The Bible is difficult in Hebrew! The Bible is difficult in Greek! The Bible is difficult in Latin! The Bible is just plain difficult!!" **Because the *Douay-Rheims Bible* is also difficult, we have, *by that fact alone*, a positive indication that it is a faithful translation of the original—which has exactly the same characteristic!** If the Bible in English is not somewhat difficult, you can be sure the Bible has not been accurately rendered into English. **RIGHT! If it is not hard, it is NOT the Bible!** But rather, it is some "gloss," where the subtle and powerful meanings that lie imbedded in the text of Sacred Scripture have been "creamed over," like some French dish covered with a sauce that obscures the flavor of the original!

Regarding the difficulty of Sacred Scripture, Saint Augustine, one of the two greatest Doctors of the Church, has observed:

> I am convinced this whole situation was ordained by God in order to overcome pride by work and restrain from haughtiness our minds, which usually disdain anything they have learned easily . . . The Holy Ghost, therefore, has generously and advantageously planned Holy Scripture in such a way that in the easier passages He relieves our hunger; in the ones that are harder to understand, He drives away our pride. Practically nothing is dug out from those unintelligible texts which is not discovered to be said very plainly in another place . . . (*On Christian Doctrine*. Bk. 2, Chap. 6, Par. 8).

In a similar vein, the great Pope Leo XIII comments in his 1893 Encyclical *On Holy Scripture* (Paragraph 5): "For the Sacred Scripture is not like other books. Dictated by the Holy Ghost, it contains things of the deepest importance, which in many instances are most difficult and obscure. To understand and explain such things, there is always required the 'coming' of the same

Holy Spirit; that is to say, His light and His grace; and these, as the Royal Psalmist so frequently insists, are to be sought by humble prayers and guarded by holiness of life."

Even St. Peter, in commenting on the difficulty of St. Paul's Epistles, mentions how difficult *they* are in particular and how difficult Scripture is in general: "As also in all *his* [St. Paul's] epistles, speaking in them of these things; in which are certain things hard to be understood, which the unlearned and unstable wrest [turn from the proper meaning], as they do also the other scriptures, to their own destruction." (*2 Peter* 3:16).

If St. Peter (who *wrote* part of Scripture), St. Augustine (who was one of the two greatest Doctors of the Church), and Pope Leo XIII (prophesied by St. Malachy—1095-1148—as "a Light in the Heavens" because of his brilliance)—if these three all had difficulty understanding Scripture, what about the average person today? **Scripture is hard to understand because Scripture is HARD! And no modern translator is going to make it easier for you by translating God's meaning out of it and his own into it!**

He is only thereby going to make it impossible for you to understand the Bible because he is keeping it from you!

To conclude on this point, let us consider the statement of Pope Pius XII in his 1943 encyclical *The Promotion of Biblical Studies* (*Divino Afflante Spiritu*), where he refers to biblical interpreters (which can also be applied to translators): "Let them therefore by means of their knowledge of languages search out with all diligence the literal meaning of the words . . ." (Paragraph 23).

It is the thesis of this little book that this has all been very beautifully accomplished in the *Latin Vulgate*, the "official" Bible of the Catholic Church, and in the *Douay-Rheims Bible*, the classic, time-honored and only faithful English translation of the *Vulgate*. **For without the *Douay-Rheims*, the Bible in English simply does not exist in one completely accurate and trustworthy translation!** Fortunately, we still have the *Douay-Rheims Bible* available to us yet today.

A Synopsis

- The *Douay-Rheims Bible* is ***the only* traditional Catholic Bible in the English language.**

- It was translated with scrupulous accuracy from the *Latin Vulgate Bible* of St. Jerome (340-420 A.D.), which was a careful translation from the original Greek and Hebrew.

- The *Latin Vulgate Bible* was used universally in the Catholic Church (Latin Rite) for over 1500 years.

- The *Vulgate* was proclaimed "authentic" by the Council of Trent in 1546.

- That Council also proclaimed: "No one [may] dare or presume under any pretext whatsoever to reject it." (4th Ses., April 8, 1546).

- Pope Pius XII declared that this means it is "free from any error whatsoever in matters of faith and morals." (1943).

- The *Douay-Rheims Bible* received relatively minor revisions by Bishop Challoner in 1749-1752.

- It was approved by the Church many times over, including by Cardinal Gibbons in 1899.

- The *Douay-Rheims Bible* was the only Catholic English translation of Scripture commonly in use for over 200 years.

- It was used in the Catholic liturgy through approximately 1960.

- It is respectful, reverent, beautiful and a pleasure to read!

- It contains no inclusive language!

- It is the best, safest and most accurate translation of the Bible in English!

- The *Douay-Rheims Bible* is so packed with meaning that a single phrase can yield profound insight—because it was translated with great respect for every word.

- The footnotes in the *Douay-Rheims Bible* are totally Catholic and are definitely *not* the opinions of modern biblical scholars.

- The *Douay-Rheims Bible* contains those powerful, familiar Bible passages—such as "Hail, full of grace, the Lord is with thee" (*Luke* 1:28)—that are substantially different in most modern Bibles.

- Catholic literature for the past 250 years is replete with quotes from the *Douay-Rheims Bible*.

- The solemnity, profundity and penetrating truth of the Word of God really come through in this version of the Bible!

- After reading *The Douay-Rheims Bible* all other English versions will seem like "approximations" of what Scripture really says.

- *The Douay-Rheims Bible* is a joy to read, is full of surprises and really makes the Bible come alive!

- *The Douay-Rheims Bible* contains those familiar, profound and commanding Bible passages which say to all:

"THIS is Sacred Scripture!"

"Lazarus, come forth." (*John* 11:43).

"Go, and now sin no more." (*John* 8:11).

"Amen I say to thee, this day thou shalt be with me in Paradise." (*Luke* 23:43).

"What therefore God hath joined together, let no man put asunder." (*Matt.* 19:6).

"Silver and gold I have none; but what I have, I give thee: In the name of Jesus Christ of Nazareth, arise, and walk." (*Acts* 3:6).

"What manner of man is this, for the winds and the sea obey him?" (*Matt.* 8:27).

"Thou art Peter; and upon this rock I will build my church, and the gates of hell shall not prevail against it." (*Matt.* 16:18).

"For what doth it profit a man, if he gain the whole world, and suffer the loss of his own soul?" (*Matt.* 16:26).

"Did you not know, that I must be about my father's business?" (*Luke* 2:49).

"Could you not watch one hour with me?" (*Matt.* 26:40).

"For many are called, but few chosen." (*Matt.* 20:16; omitted from 8 of 9 modern Bibles reviewed here).

"Where their worm dieth not, and the fire is not extinguished." (*Mark.* 9:43; omitted from 7 of 9 modern Bibles reviewed here).

"For we are the children of saints, and we must not be joined together like heathens that know not God." (*Tobias* 8:45; and other marriage instructions from the book of *Tobias*: omitted from 9 of 9 modern Bibles reviewed here).

"For he is risen, as he said." (*Matt.* 28:6).

What Can You Do?

If you want to know, love, and help pass on the Catholic Scriptural traditions, you need to have and read the *Douay-Rheims Bible*. Everyone who understands the very important message of this little book needs to own a copy of the *Douay-Rheims Bible*.

And what about the young Catholics, the upcoming generations of Catholics?

Everyone who understands the message of this little book needs to obtain a copy of the *Douay-Rheims Bible* for each of their children and each of their grandchildren. Even if these young people do not appreciate the *Douay-Rheims Bible* now, they will thereby have a copy for a future rebirth of our Catholic Scriptural traditions. For now, they will at least treasure their *Douay-Rheims Bible* because it was given to them by Mom and Dad, or by Grandma and Grandpa—and later they will have the basic tool to rediscover their Catholic Scriptural heritage.

Our Catholic Scriptural tradition is part of our Catholic culture and is something that must be handed on to the next generation as a living tradition—along with our living Catholic traditions of doctrine, moral teaching, liturgy and devotions. All these elements form a bond of unity among Catholics today, and between us and our Catholic forebears, the Saints. If the continuity of our Scriptural tradition gets broken (as it *has*, in many cases), how will it ever get re-established?

Let's keep our Catholic Scriptural tradition alive and strong. PASS IT ON!

The clergy and hierarchy have their hands full with many other battles in this secular time. But the laity can play an essential role in preserving and handing on our Catholic Scriptural tradition. The first step is:

1. Get a DOUAY-RHEIMS BIBLE for yourself.
2. Give a DOUAY-RHEIMS BIBLE to every one of your children.
3. Give a DOUAY-RHEIMS BIBLE to every one of your grandchildren.
4. Give a DOUAY-RHEIMS BIBLE to anyone else who should have one!

Let us as Catholics look forward to the day when the Catholic world will rediscover the treasure it possesses in the *Douay-Rheims Bible*. Let us work toward the day when the *Douay-Rheims Bible* will become once again the universal heritage of Catholics throughout the entire English-speaking world.

—ORDER FORM—

Gentlemen:

Please send me __________ copy (copies) of **The Douay-Rheims Bible**.

☐ Enclosed is my payment in the amount of _______ .

☐ Please charge to ☐ Visa ☐ MasterCard ☐ Discover

Credit Card No. ______________________________

My credit card expires ___________________________

Name ______________________________________

Street ______________________________________

City _______________________________________

State ________________________ Zip ___________

All orders shipped promptly. U.S. customers, please add shipping and handling on each order going to one address in the following amounts: For orders of $1-$10, add $3.00; $10.01-$25, add $5.00; $25.01-$50, add $6.00; $50.01-$75, add $7.00; $75.01-$150.00, add $8.00; orders of $150.01 or more, add $10.00. Illinois residents please add 6% sales tax. All foreign and Canadian customers please remit in U.S. funds payable thru a U.S. bank. Overseas customers please call or email us for exact freight. VISA, MasterCard, and Discover welcome. For fastest service, phone, FAX or e-mail your order any time. FAX: 815-226-7770. You can also order thru our Website: www.tanbooks.com. Tel. Toll Free: 1-800-437-5876. Sales people are on duty Mon.-Fri.: 7 a.m.–Midnight; Sat.: 8 a.m.–6 p.m., Central Time. Leave a recorded order with your address, phone number and credit card number at any other time.

Toll Free 1-800-437-5876

FAX 815-226-7770 **www.tanbooks.com**

TAN BOOKS AND PUBLISHERS, INC.
P.O. Box 424 • Rockford, Illinois 61105